ACCLAIM FOR NO CROSS, NO CROWN

"This contemporary version of *No Cross, No Crown* provides a great reminder of William Penn's influence in the founding of the United States, and, more importantly, Penn's timeless message of our individual need to be on fire for Christ."

—Alan R. Garner
President & CEO, Volunteers of America of Pennsylvania

"Pennsylvania's beautiful capitol building honors our Commonwealth's founder, William Penn, both with a mosaic of his famous prayer, that God would make his land "the seed of a nation," and with a set of murals depicting his faith conversion and voyage to the New World. Now, through this modern translation of his book, *No Cross, No Crown*, we are afforded a deeper look at this great man. What a gift!"

—Michael Geer,
President, Pennsylvania Family Institute

"*No Cross, No Crown* is a timeless adventure into the words and thoughts of William Penn. His vast, spiritual knowledge provides an inspiring, educational, and motivating study of Christ and his cross."

—Donna Watson, PhD
Author

NO CROSS, NO CROWN

A Discourse Showing

the Nature and Discipline of the Holy Cross of Christ

and that the Denial of Self and Daily Bearing of Christ's Cross

Is the Only Way to the Rest and Kingdom of God

by

William Penn

Founder and Owner of the Colony of Pennsylvania

1682

www.TheGreatChallenge.info

ISBN 978-1-4675-2613-5

Cover and interior design by Heidi Lowe

Printed by Litho Printers & Bindery
Cassville, Missouri

Library of Congress information pending.

ISBN 978-146752613-5

The Great Challenge

"THE GREAT CHALLENGE" is for those who profess to be "Christians." Each one must examine himself or herself with this soul-searching question:

WHERE AM *I* WITH JESUS?

Jesus said, "If anyone wants to follow me, he must carry his cross every day. He must say no to himself and follow me" (Luke 9:23).

Later Jesus said, "I know what you've done. You are not cold; you are not hot. I wish you were either cold or hot! Instead, you are lukewarm—not hot, not cold. So, I am going to vomit you out of my mouth" (Rev. 3:15-16).

So, which one am I? (check one)

❑ HOT

❑ COLD

❑ LUKEWARM

William Penn quoted many Scriptures to help us understand how we can be "HOT" for Jesus. He was severely persecuted for publicly disagreeing with the official Church of England. (That was illegal back then.) Hopefully, you will come to appreciate the tough times in which he lived His conscience told him that he belonged to Jesus, not to any man-made institution!

After reading this book, *No Cross, No Crown*, will I accept "the Great Challenge"?

Pledge: I hereby take "the Great Challenge" to find out whether I am truly "in the faith" or not. (See Acts 14:22; 16:5; 1 Cor. 16:13; 2 Cor. 13:5; Col. 1:23; 2:7; 1 Tim. 3:13; Titus 1:13; 1 Pet. 5:9.)

Name: _____

Date: _____

UNLESS YOU PICK UP YOUR CROSS EVERY DAY FOR JESUS, YOU CANNOT EXPECT TO RECEIVE A CROWN IN HEAVEN!

Contents

A Short Introduction xii

A History of the Life of William Penn xv

William Penn's Preface 1

Chapter 1 — What it Takes to be a Real Christian 5

Chapter 2 — Keep on Following Christ...............................19

Chapter 3 — Is It *Your* Cross? 31

Chapter 4 — Worshiping God...53

Chapter 5 — A New Attitude 67

PRIDE

Chapter 6 — The Wrong Kind of Pride................................95

Chapter 7 — Humility vs. Pride... 111

Chapter 8 — The Characteristics of Pride 139

GREED

Chapter 9 — Covetousness... 157

MATERIALISM

Chapter 10— "Eat, Drink, and Be Merry"........................ 177

Chapter 11— You and "The World" 195

Chapter 12— Leaving "Babylon" Behind.......................... 209

The Editor's Note

THIS NEW EDITION OF *No Cross, No Crown* is an entirely new translation of William Penn's original 2nd edition published in 1682. The English language has undergone tremendous changes over the last 300 years or so. In addition, even in his own day, Penn's frilly, repetitive style was very difficult for his readers to comprehend. Here is a sample of Penn's original wording in 1682:

> But alas! what is the reason that the cry is so common, Must we always dote on these things? Why most certainly it is this, they know not what is the joy and peace of speaking and acting, as in the presence of the most holy God that passeth such vain understandings (Eph. 4:18-20): darkened with the glories and pleasures of the god of this world (2 Cor. 4:4); whose religion is so many mumbling and ignorantly devout said words, as they teach parrots; for if they were of those whose hearts are set on things above, and whose treasure is in heaven, there would their minds inhabit, and their greatest pleasure constantly be: and such who call that a burden, and seek to be refreshed by such pastimes as a play, a morrice-dance, a punchinello,

a ball, a masque, cards, dice, or the like, I am bold to affirm, they not only never knew the divine excellency of God and his truth, but thereby declare themselves most unfit for them in another world. For how is it possible that they can be delighted to eternity with that satisfaction, which is so tedious and irksome for thirty or forty years, that, for a supply of recreation to their minds, the little toys and fopperies of this perishing world must be brought into practice and request?

Now, here is the same sample translated into Modern English:

But this is such a common complaint: "Why must we always dwell on these things?" Because many do not know the joy of being in the presence of God (Eph. 4:18-20). This surpasses all vain understandings (Rom. 10:2) which are darkened with the glories and pleasures of the god of this world (2 Cor. 4:4). If they were people whose hearts are set on things above (Col. 3:1-4), and whose treasure is in heaven (Matt. 6:20), then their minds would be in the right place. Those who call this a "burden" and seek to be refreshed by vain pastimes have never known God and His truth. They are declaring themselves to be most unfit for Him in another world. For, how is it possible that they can be satisfied for eternity with what is so tedious and irksome for 30 or 40 years!?

The translators have done their best to preserve the sense of Penn's original meaning within his culture. Sometimes, wherever possible, they were able to retain actual words or phrases that came from his own hand.

There were 18 chapters in the 1682 edition, but the translators decided to combine the content of those chapters into 12 chapters by grouping them according to similar subject matter. Originally, Penn's Chapter 10 was entitled "Thee and Thou to Single Persons." This chapter was deleted because it is now irrelevant for a modern audience. Regarding the use of pronouns, in English today, there is *no* distinction between "thee/thou" and "you." But in Penn's day, the Quakers insisted that it was pride that demanded that the word "you" be used when referring to high-ranking officials, and "thee" or "thou" was to be used for persons of equal rank or those who were below one's rank.

We are assuming that William Penn, who was very familiar with his Bible, was quoting from the King James Version, which first appeared in 1611. In this new edition of *No Cross, No Crown*, all Scripture quotations are taken from the *International English*™ *Bible* (copyright © 2012. All Rights Reserved.). This is a new modern translation of the whole Bible. Permission was granted by:

International Bible Translators, Inc.
P.O. Box 6203
Branson, MO 65615

A Short Introduction

ABOUT 2,000 YEARS AGO, Jesus made a shocking statement to some so-called "Christians" in Laodicea. Jesus sent a special letter to them through the Apostle John. It said, "I know what you've done. You are not cold; you are not hot. I wish you were either cold or hot! Instead, you are luke-warm—not hot, not cold. So, I am going to vomit you out of my mouth" (Rev. 3:15-16).

I know what "cold" means, and I know what "lukewarm" means, but what does "hot" mean? What did Jesus mean by that term?

Was the Apostle Peter "hot" for Jesus? He thought so. On the night when Jesus was arrested, Peter claimed, "Lord, I am ready to go to jail with you. I will even die with you!" (Luke 22:33). But what happened later that same night? Three times he denied knowing Jesus (Luke 22:54-61). Later, after the resurrection of Christ, Jesus told him: "I am telling you the truth, Peter, when you were young, you tied your own belt and you walked where you wanted to go. But when you get old, you will stretch out your hands and someone else will tie you.[1] They will carry you where

---

1   To crucify Peter. This occurred in Rome.

you don't want to go." (Jesus said this to show what kind of death would be used to bring glory to God.) After Jesus said this, he said to Peter, "Follow me!" (John 21:17-18). A few years later, Peter's new-found commitment was put to the test when he was arrested by King Herod, and Peter was going to be executed the next morning (Acts 12:1-19).

And, what about Paul? What kind of a man was he? When he opposed the little band of Jewish Christians whose "heresy" about Jesus was starting to spread, Paul was certainly what we would call "hot" (Acts 8:1-3)! But he was "hot" for the wrong thing. In fact, you could call him a fanatic. He wasn't satisfied with persecuting those "non-conformists" in Jerusalem, he wanted to root them out in other cities, like Damascus which is about 135 miles northeast of Jerusalem. He got some letters from the Jewish authorities in Jerusalem to go up there and drag them back to Jerusalem for a trial. But something dramatic happened on the way—he met Jesus (Acts 9:1-19). And that experience changed his life forever!

Would you say that Paul was "hot" for Jesus then? Yes, he was. Look how the Lord turned Paul's life around in Damascus (Acts 9:20-25)!

So many times Paul was tested (2 Cor. 11:22-33). He wrote a bunch of letters in prison. Just before Paul died, he wrote his last letter to young Timothy, his faithful companion. Paul said, "For I am now ready to be offered, and the time of my departure is at hand. I have fought a good fight. I have finished my course. I have kept the faith. Henceforth, there is laid up for me a *crown* of righteousness, which the Lord, the righteous judge, shall give me at that day. And not to me only, but unto all them also that love his appearing" (2 Tim. 4:6-8, KJV). Soon after that, the Romans chopped off Paul's head.

Jesus said, "Be faithful, even if you must die. I will give you the *crown* of life" (Rev. 2:10, KJV).

A History of the Life of William Penn

SOME INTERESTING FACTS

WHAT DO YOU KNOW ABOUT WILLIAM PENN?

Did you know that . . . ?

- He was way ahead of his time.

- He was once the largest, private landholder in America.

- He was America's first great champion of democracy and religious freedom.

- He set forth the democratic principles that served as an inspiration for the U.S. Constitution.

- As one of the earlier supporters of colonial unification, Penn wrote and urged for a union of all the English colonies. (This later became the United States of America!)

NO CROSS, NO CROWN

- He gave Pennsylvania a written constitution that limited the power of government.

- He guaranteed many fundamental liberties.

- He established a sanctuary in the New World that protected one's freedom of conscience.

- He offered equal rights to people of different races and religions

- He spoke several languages.

- He insisted that women deserved equal rights with men.

- He provided for a humane prison system.

- He drafted a comprehensive plan for a United States of Europe.

THE POWER OF ONE

THOSE WERE SOME REMARKABLE accomplishments for just one man! Although Benjamin Franklin usually gets more attention, it was William Penn who preceded him and deserves at least equal rank among the most remarkable men who have ever lived.

By creating Pennsylvania, William Penn set an enormously important example for liberty. He showed that people who are courageous enough, persistent enough, and resourceful enough *can* live free. He went beyond the natural rights theories of his philosopher friend, John Locke, and showed how a free society would actually work. He showed how individuals of different races and religions *can* live together peacefully when they mind their own business. He affirmed the optimism of free people. Pennsylvania had many of the rights and liberties that would later be granted to the citizens of the United States after 1776.

What a life Penn lived! Was he an American? No, he wasn't. But he set the stage for what was to become America, a freedom-loving country. He visited his colony several times, but he ended up dying back in England. You see, he lived long before some of our founding fathers in America, like Benjamin Franklin, Thomas Jefferson, Patrick Henry, and Tom Paine. Our

Declaration of Independence and the U.S. Constitution would never have been written if it had not been for the influence of William Penn. But, I'm getting ahead of myself.

HIS PARENTS

LET'S GO BACK TO the beginning of William's life. He was born on Oct. 14, 1644 in London, England and raised in the privileged Tower Hill section of town. Like most everyone else, his parents were Anglicans (English Catholic). His mother was Margaret Jasper, a widow of a Dutch sea captain. She was raised in Rotterdam, Holland as the daughter of an English business agent. And his father was Sir William Penn, Sr., who was seldom home because he lived on the high seas for years at a time, like his father before him. Penn Sr. was in great demand because he knew the waters around England extremely well. He could handle a ship in bad weather and always got the most out of his crew. He was eventually promoted to Admiral in the Royal Navy. And William Penn, Jr. was his only son, an only child.

Around the age of 12 in Ireland, at his father's castle, young William met a man named Thomas Loe who touched his heart with the simple message of Jesus. It was compelling. William never forgot that. About a decade later, he met up with Mr. Loe again. This time William started getting "hot" for Jesus.

HIS TEEN YEARS

BUT WILLIAM JR. HAD a rebellious streak in his teenage years. At Oxford he didn't want to be forced to go to chapel or wear the church uniform. He got kicked out of school at the age of 17. This enraged his father. It was embarrassing. His father attacked young Penn with his cane and forced him out of his home. But Penn's mother made peace in the family and allowed her son to return home. However, she quickly concluded that both her social standing and her husband's career could be threatened by her son's behavior. So at age 18, young Penn was sent off to Paris to get him out of the country, to improve his manners, and to expose him to another culture. You see, his father wanted the boy to be able to win favor in the court of King Charles II (1630-1685) (as he had done).

In France the boy attended the most respected French Protestant University. While there, he met Moise Amyraut, a Christian humanist who supported religious tolerance. He believed in free will (unlike the somber Puritans back in England with their rigid beliefs and crippling guilt). Penn studied with Amyraut for one year. Penn was encouraged to search for his own religious path. This encounter began to shape his thinking about his fellow man. The extravagant display of wealth and privilege of the court of Louis XIV did not sit well with young Penn. He was also very uncomfortable with Catholic ritual. When William Penn, Jr. returned to England two years later, he was a handsome, sophisticated, well-mannered, young man. Here is a portrait of what he looked like about that time.

William Penn, Jr. caught the pox at a young age and he lost all of his hair. So he wore a wig until he left college.

For a while, the Admiral used his son as a special courier to deliver secret military messages directly to King Charles II (1630-1685). That's how young William got to know the king so well. (That would be an important contact for him later.) He also became acquainted with the Duke of York, who would later become King James II (1633-1701).

In 1665 London was in the grip of the bubonic plague. Young Penn reflected on the intense suffering and the massive deaths. He noticed the way human beings reacted during the widespread epidemic. Penn wrote in his diary: "(This pestilence) gave me a deep sense of the vanity of this world, of the irreligiousness of the religions in it." He noticed how the Quakers were very compassionate during those days, but they were regarded as criminals by the authorities. They were often arrested by the police and vilified. The Quakers were even accused of causing the plague! William Penn decided to become a Quaker.

IN THE TOWER OF LONDON

SOON AFTER THAT TIME, William fell in love with Gulielma Springett, and after a 4-year engagement they were married in 1672. They had 7 children (but 4 of them died in infancy). She died in 1694 around the age of 50.

But again, I'm getting a little ahead of myself. This book, *No Cross, No Crown*, was written when William Penn was in prison! The king's men had had enough of Penn's troublesome, political pamphlets, and one in particular—*The Shaky Foundation Shaken*. He was attacking major church doctrines of the Church of England. The Bishop of London ordered that Penn be held indefinitely, until he publicly recanted his written statements. The official charge was "publication without a license" but the real crime was "blasphemy" (as signed in a warrant by King Charles II). Young Penn also refused to swear an oath of allegiance to the king of England (because of what it says in Matt. 5:34). He wouldn't even take his hat off to the king as a sign of respect.

So, in 1668 the British authorities threw William Penn into the Tower of London in an unheated cell in solitary confinement. He was threatened with a life sentence! But Penn was given plenty of paper and lots of ink to write a retraction of what he had said in *The Shaky Foundation Shaken*. But Penn said, "My prison will be my grave before I will budge a jot, for I owe my conscience to no mortal man!" That was when he wrote this inflammatory book, *No Cross, No Crown*. But they let him go after 8 months, and his conscience hadn't really changed. He is also famous for saying: "Right is right, even if everyone is against it; and wrong is wrong, even if everyone is for it!" His protests against the state church and the government were just beginning.

Young Penn was sprung from jail because of his family's rank more than by his principles. His father called for him and said, "What's wrong with you!?" The Admiral was very upset by his son's actions. His father had hoped that his son's charisma and intelligence would win the young man favor in the court of the king. But now his plans for his son were crushed. Though upset, the old Admiral tried his best to reason with his son, but it didn't do any good. His father feared for his own position, too. His son was on a dangerous course which might be at odds with the crown! But young Penn was more determined than ever. So, Sir William Penn felt that he had no choice but to order his son out of the house and to withhold his inheritance!

Young Penn was now homeless. He lived with several Quaker families. Unlike the Puritans, the Quakers had *no* political agenda. But they sincerely believed that every individual was *equal* under God. But this contradicted the absolute position of the royal family of England; the monarchy was thought to be divinely appointed by God. In those days, all minority groups were treated as "heretics" because of their principles and their failure to pay tithes to the Church of England. They also refused to swear oaths of loyalty to the King.

HIS LEGAL BATTLES

WILLIAM PENN WAS ARRESTED six times for speaking out courageously against intolerance. He was always advocating personal rights, property rights, and religious rights. Among the most famous of these arrests was his trial for preaching on the street in 1670. (He was getting "hotter" for Jesus.) But Penn had studied common law and courtroom strategy in London back in 1664, and he was quite capable of challenging oppressive, government policies in court. He was an eloquent speaker and a prolific writer. His penetrating insights into the very basics of English law are still taught in law schools today. It turns out that Penn displayed a towering legal mind, and he won several big lawsuits.

In this particular case, he pleaded for his right to see a copy of the charges which were being laid out against him and the laws that he had allegedly broken. But the judge, the Lord Mayor of London, refused, even though this right was guaranteed by English law. The judge was not presenting a formal indictment. Furthermore, the judge directed the jury to come to a verdict *without* hearing the defense! Despite heavy pressure from the Lord Mayor to convict the man, the jury returned a verdict of "not guilty." When invited by the judge to reconsider their verdict and to select a new foreman, the jury refused. They were all sent to cells for several nights to mull over their "decision." The judge said to them, "You shall go together and bring in another verdict, or you shall starve!" The Lord Mayor sent Penn to Newgate Prison on a charge of contempt of court. But the jury wouldn't change their decision. So the Lord Mayor sent the entire jury to the same jail, and he fined each of them one year's wages. From this brutal prison, the members of that jury fought their case. It was called Bushell's Case.

Two months later, the Court of Common Pleas issued a writ of *habeas corpus*[1] to set them free. They had managed to win the right for *all* English juries to be free from the control of judges. This case was one of the more important trials in British history. It shaped the future concept of freedom in America, too.

Then that same jury sued Lord Mayor of London for false arrest. After that, the Lord Chief Justice of England, along with his 11 fellow-judges,

---

1 This is a document which demands that a prisoner be given an immediate hearing or else be released.

ruled unanimously that juries must *not* be coerced or punished for their verdicts. Finally, the right to a trial by jury was protected.

"THE HOLY EXPERIMENT"

IN THE MEANTIME, WITH his father dying, young Penn wanted to see him one more time and to patch up their differences. But he urged his father *not* to pay his fine and free him: "I entreat thee not to purchase my liberty." But the Admiral refused to let that opportunity pass by. The old man paid the fine, thereby releasing his son from jail.

Over time, the old man gained respect for his son's integrity and courage. The Admiral told him, "Let nothing in this world tempt you to wrong your conscience." Knowing that after his death, young Penn would become more vulnerable in his pursuit of justice, the Admiral reinstated William Penn, Jr.'s inheritance. So, the son suddenly came into a large fortune. This significant act not only secured his son's protection but also set the conditions for the founding of Pennsylvania. The Admiral wrote to the Duke of York (the successor to the throne), requesting from the crown that, in return for the Admiral's lifetime service to King Charles II, the royal family would promise to shield young Penn and make him "a royal counselor." They agreed to do so.

Later, with the blessing of both King Charles II and the Duke of York, William Penn presented his case for religious tolerance before Parliament, but it was rejected. So, conditions for minorities were deteriorating.

After this, Penn became convinced that religious tolerance could *not* be achieved in England. He had dreamed of his "Holy Experiment" in which he could establish a utopian, American colony where there would be a *guaranteed* freedom of religion.

So William Penn, Jr. proposed a solution which would solve the dilemma—a mass emigration of English Quakers to the New World. Some Quakers had already moved to North America, but the New England

Puritans were just as hostile toward Quakers as the Anglicans were in England. And some of the Quakers had already been banished to the Caribbean. In 1677, a group of prominent Quakers (which included young Penn) purchased the colonial province of West Jersey (half of the current State of New Jersey). With the New Jersey foothold in place, Penn pressed his case to extend the Quaker region in America. So, Penn went straight to King Charles II and asked for a charter. And, surprisingly, he got it. It happened on March 4, 1681.

The King of England granted an extraordinarily generous charter to William Penn, Jr. Young Penn had all rights and privileges as the sole pro- prietor. (He could do anything but declare war.) The following day Penn was jubilant. He wrote in his diary: "It is a clear and just thing, and my God who has given it to me through many difficulties, will, I believe, bless and make it the seed of a nation." (He continued to get "hotter" for Jesus.)

The charter provided for the territory west of the Delaware River and north of Maryland. There were already about one thousand people there— some Germans, some Dutch people, and a few native Indians. But there was no real government present. No doubt, the king thought that this was a good way to get rid of most of the dissidents that were causing him so much trouble in England.

The background behind this large purchase is interesting: William Penn, Sr. had served in the Commonwealth Navy during the English Civil War and was rewarded by Oliver Cromwell with land estates in Ireland. But the lands were seized from Irish Catholics in retaliation for an earlier massacre of Protestants. After Cromwell died, the royalists resurged. The middle class aligned itself with the royalists and Admiral Penn was sent on a secret mission to bring back exiled Prince Charles. For his role in re- storing the monarchy, Admiral Penn was knighted and gained a powerful position as Commissioner of the Navy. The crown was re-established, but King Charles II still harassed and persecuted all religions and sects other than the Anglican Church.

Once the Penn family returned to England from Ireland, King Charles

NO CROSS, NO CROWN

II owed the Admiral a whole lot of money for helping to reinstate him as king. It was the Admiral's back pay. So a proposal was made for the king to pay off this debt. It was £16,000. The king cancelled this debt by transferring to him 45,000 square miles of land in the New World. That was bigger than all of England! (That tract of land is now eastern New Jersey, Delaware, and Pennsylvania). William Penn, Jr. would become the largest, private landowner in American history. The king suggested that it should be called "Pennsylvania"[2] out of respect to Sir William Penn Sr.

So young William Penn received that special charter to be the proprietor of a new colony of Englishmen in the New World. On Nov. 8, 1682, he set sail on the ship called "Welcome" to go see it. The voyage took 8 weeks. Many of the passengers fell sick and died on the way. A compassionate Penn volunteered to help them. (He was getting "hotter" for Jesus.) During that same year, he revised his book, *No Cross, No Crown*, which he had written when he was in prison back in 1668.[3]

THE NEW COLONY

WILLIAM PENN WAS BOTH idealistic and practical. He loved to soar, but he had the good sense to pull back, too. He was pragmatic. He worked hard to write *The First Frame of Government*, a legal basis for a free society. (It took over 20 drafts.) It was the first constitution. Amazingly, it *limited* the power of government. And, through amendments, it allowed for peaceful change, but any amendment could only be passed by both the consent of the Governor and 85 percent of the elected representatives. And citizens had the right to own private property. This is some of the wording of that

2 "Sylvania" is Latin for "woods" or "forest".

3 And that is the edition which you will be reading in the pages of this book. He quoted 68 other classical authors (from memory!) who agreed with his principles, but very few people today would know who those people were. That is why they were deleted from this edition. We wanted to keep it as short as possible.

historic document: "Men being born with a title to perfect freedom and uncontrolled enjoyment of all the rights and privileges of the law of nature. . . . No one can be put out of his estate and subjected to the political view of another without his consent."

Penn himself would be the Governor, and there would be a Council of 72 members which would propose legislation, and then a General Assembly (up to 500 members), which could either approve or defeat proposed legislation. Each year, one-third of the members would be elected for 3-year terms. Governor William Penn retained a veto over any proposed legislation. This form of government provided for virtually unlimited free enterprise, a free press, trial by jury, and religious tolerance. Back in England, the death penalty was given for 200 offenses, but Penn reserved the death penalty for only two crimes—murder and treason. He insisted on low taxes, too. He even suspended all taxes for a year to help promote settlements. The final version of their constitution which was adopted in 1701 lasted for 75 years, and it became the basis of Pennsylvania's state constitution (adopted in 1776).

Penn also drew up a detailed design for an entire city. It was going to be called "Philadelphia" (which means, "The City of Brotherly Love" in Greek). Under his direction, the city of Philadelphia was carefully planned and developed. Penn wanted to build a 10,000-acre city, but his friends thought that was overly optimistic. He settled for 1,200 acres to start with. Penn wanted 80-acre gentleman's estates to surround the core of the city. Each of these mansions was to be set apart by at least 800 feet from its neighbor and surrounded by fields and gardens—a sort of greenbelt that encircled the metropolis, like a modern suburb. Strangely, there was no military draft. Quakers were pacifists.

People from everywhere flocked to Penn's new colony (Jews, Catholics, the Irish, the Welsh, Lutherans, some Dutch, Swedes, Finns, Mennonites, the Amish, Huguenots, Dunkers, Moravians, Pietists, and Schwenkfelders). Pennsylvania was developing into a successful "melting pot."

They liked Penn's concept of freedom very much. He advocated that "all men are created equal."Penn had a saying: "Men must be governed by God, or they will be ruled by tyrants." He wrote: "No men . . . hath power or authority to rule over men's consciences in religious matters." Penn guaranteed free and fair trials by jury, progressive prisons, freedom of religion, freedom from unjust imprisonment, free elections, and a separation of powers. The laws of public behavior that Penn laid out were rather Puritanical though—no swearing, lying, or drunkenness. "Idle amusements" such as stage plays, gambling, carousing, masquerade parties, cockfighting, and bear-baiting were forbidden.

Penn vigorously marketed the colony throughout Europe in various languages. He wanted everybody to come to America. Penn was very convincing, too. He persuaded many emigrants from several nations to take the dangerous, ocean passage to settle in the New World. And he persuaded speculators to invest in property there. Penn planned to make money by selling tracts of land, and, although he was able to attract a good number of investors, he never realized the financial profits that he imagined.

DEALING WITH THE INDIANS

WHO WAS THIS YOUNG, aristocratic governor? Was he a religious freak? After the building plans for Philadelphia had been completed and Penn's political ideas had been put into a workable form, he explored the interior of his colony.

He was a realist. He would not permit any white settlers to come into his lands until peace treaties with the Indians were in place. And, William Penn insisted on paying the Indians a fair price for their land—even if that meant buying the land three times over!

Penn befriended the local Indians, primarily the Delaware tribe. He even learned several different Indian dialects in order to negotiate directly with them without interpreters! Penn was tall, good looking, and very athletic. (Back in England he would often run 3 miles to school.) Here in

America he walked unarmed and unafraid among the Indians. They were impressed that he could outrun any of them. He always treated them with respect. He is famous for his "Great Treaty" with the Indians. Penn's various treaties with most of the Indians lasted for seven decades. The Indians were at peace with the colonists of Pennsylvania much longer than any other English colony because of Penn's fairness.

TROUBLE BACK IN ENGLAND

BUT THERE WERE PROBLEMS that needed his immediate attention back in England. He had to appear in court in 1684 against Lord Baltimore over a border dispute between their two colonies—Maryland and Pennsylvania. Lord Baltimore was controlling the territory south of Pennsylvania. Penn had not taken the simple step of determining exactly where the 40th degree of latitude actually was. Under Penn's charter, it was supposed to be the southern boundary of his land. But dissension arose between the two proprietors after Penn sent letters to several landowners in Maryland advising them that they were probably in Pennsylvania and that they didn't have to pay any more taxes to Lord Baltimore.

And, the political climate in England was changing. Internal political conflicts there even threatened to revoke his Pennsylvania charter. William Penn was going to need to use all his charm and grace to persuade the king to release some political prisoners as well. Some of Penn's religious friends had been thrown into prison, and a few of them had even been executed. So, Penn intervened diplomatically with his old friend, the Duke of York (who was now named King James II after his brother King Charles II died in 1685). Penn saved quite a number of Quakers from the gallows.

The England of the 1690's was a tumultuous place, especially for an outspoken, liberal Quaker like William Penn. But he never backed away from a political fight. But his forthrightness was dangerous. Because Penn had supported James II (and James II (a Stuart king) was dethroned by

William III and Queen Mary), Penn was automatically suspected of treason. He was arrested by the government. And, the British government seized his estates. Penn was eventually cleared of all charges but he was still tainted as a "traitor." For the next 4 years he was a fugitive in London, hiding everywhere in the slum sections. That is why Penn lost some control over his colony briefly from 1692 to 1694. And he received another setback. His dear wife "Guli" died in 1694. It was his good friend John Locke who helped to restore his good name.

Almost two years later, William Penn married a much younger woman named Hannah Callowhill. His spirit revived. He was 52 years old, and she was around 25. She would give birth to 8 more children in a dozen years, but the first 2 died in infancy.

GOVERNOR PENN RETURNED TO HIS COLONY

IN 1699 WILLIAM PENN returned to Pennsylvania, the English colony that he owned. To his delight, he found that it was flourishing—18,000 people had settled there. Philadelphia, had now grown to a population of about 3,000 people. His previously-planted trees were everywhere. Philadelphia was now a big seaport. Sometimes more than 100 trading ships were anchored in its harbor on any given day. The people enjoyed all sorts of imported goods that came from England. America was now a viable market for English wares. And, most importantly to Penn, religious diversity was succeeding. There was an educated work force and a high literacy rate. Many were learned in science and medicine. Banks thrived, but the province still had not turned a profit. Penn was too soft. He couldn't seem to collect the taxes which were due to him. People wanted to pay him in barter instead of cash. Merchants were much more interested in making money than in his pacifist theology.

But the Quakers were beginning to retreat from the mainstream of the colony. The budding commonwealth was becoming more and more "worldly" all the time. After Penn's death, Pennsylvania slowly drifted away from being a colony that was founded on religion to a secular state dominated by commerce. Many of Penn's legal and political innovations took root, however. Fifty years after his death, the Pennsylvania Quakers withdrew from politics entirely. They were unable to run a pacifist colony without William Penn.

Unfortunately, during Penn's long absence from his colony, political squabbling had set in. Changes in local leadership had taken place. In what is now Delaware, Penn's Quaker government was not viewed favorably by the Dutch, the Swedish, or the English settlers. Those people had no "historical" allegiance to Pennsylvania. So, almost immediately, they began petitioning for their own separate Assembly. In 1691 a man named George Keith also led a religious division, and this caused "Pennsylvania" and "Delaware" to separate into two provinces. In 1704 the residents of "Delaware" finally achieved their goal. The three southernmost counties were permitted to split off from "Pennsylvania" and become the new semi-autonomous colony of "Lower Delaware." New Castle was the most prominent, prosperous and influential city in that new colony, so it became their new capital.

Their "Charter of Privileges" allowed the Assembly greater autonomy. This new charter governed the people until the American Revolution occurred. It effectively gave voters more power than Penn had by eliminating the Upper House (which represented mostly the wealthy class). Also, Jews and non-Christians were barred from holding public office.

Back in 1696, the charter of William Markham (Penn's secretary and then governor of Delaware) had replaced the earlier *Frame*. However, when Penn returned in 1701, he revised that version of it. By the time Penn left in November of that year, the colony's Assembly was elected yearly and enjoyed a more powerful position than the Governor, who, despite his veto power, was secondary in importance to their legislative body.

Penn yearned to remain in the New World, wanting to settle down in his beloved Pennsbury estate (up the Delaware River a little ways from

Philadelphia), but there were even more political problems back in England which forced his return there. So Penn went back home to face some very expensive legal battles. Some of his opponents were trying to convert his province into a colony directly ruled by the crown. But Queen Anne received Penn favorably, and he was able to retain his holdings in America.

THE LAST PART OF WILLIAM PENN'S LIFE

PENN'S LATTER YEARS WERE clouded by debt and illness. Penn had some surprises in store for him when he got back to England. Immediately he became swamped in financial and family troubles. His oldest son (William) was leading a wild life, neglecting his wife and two children and running up huge gambling debts. Penn had hoped that this son would succeed him in America, but now Penn could not even pay his son's debts. And, Penn's own finances were in shambles. He had sunk over £30,000 in America and received very little back except in the form of some bartered goods. Penn had also made many generous loans, but he couldn't collect on them.

The end of Penn's life was a tragedy of betrayal. He never cared much about money, though he had lots and lots of it. He treated his Pennsylvania property as sort of a hobby. He was so immensely rich that he could afford to lose money on it. He was just too idealistic to bother himself with the details of business. Over the course of his lifetime, his settlements always lost money, and William Penn subsidized them generously from his other assets. Although Penn exhibited a remarkable organizational talent, his management skill was mostly lax, his judgment of agents often proved too trusting, and he permitted himself to be exploited by poorly-designed contracts which led to his eventual financial ruin. William Penn's sloppiness eventually caught up with him.

One of Penn's closest friends betrayed him. He was a fellow Quaker. His name was Philip Ford. Ford embezzled very large sums from Penn's estates. Ford cheated Penn out of thousands of British pounds by concealing and diverting rents from Penn's Irish lands, claiming losses, then extracting loans from Penn to cover the shortfall. Penn never suspected that this was going on. Penn would often sign papers without even reading them. But one of the papers turned out to be a deed transferring *all* of Pennsylvania to Ford! Then Ford later demanded full rent from Penn!!

To make matters worse, after Ford died in 1702, Ford's widow (Bridget) threatened to sell all of Pennsylvania (to which she could prove that she had the title). Penn sent his son William to America to manage affairs but he proved to be just as unreliable as he had been in England.

At that time, there were considerable discussions about scrapping Penn's constitution altogether. In desperation, Penn tried to sell the Pennsylvania colony back to the crown (before Bridget Ford got wind of his plan). However, because Penn insisted that the crown should uphold the civil liberties that had been achieved, he could *not* strike a deal with the king. Mrs. Ford took her case to court. She succeeded in convincing the court to incarcerate William Penn. At age 62, Penn landed in debtors' prison! However, the court's sympathy reduced Penn's punishment to house arrest. When a group of Quakers arranged for Ford's estate to receive a payment for back rent, Penn was released from jail. Later, in 1708 Mrs. Ford was finally denied her claim to Pennsylvania! The Lord Chancellor ruled in Penn's favor.

In 1712 William Penn suffered a stroke. Four months later, he suffered a second stroke, and he was unable to take care of himself. He had difficulty speaking and writing. He could never leave England again. Slowly he lost his memory.

His wife Hannah managed all of his affairs until he died on July 30, 1718. He was 73 years old. He died penniless. She was the sole executor of his estate. She became the *de facto* governor of Pennsylvania.

After Hannah's death in 1726 the proprietorship of Pennsylvania passed on to their three sons. Their names were John, Thomas, and Richard. His sons renounced the Quaker faith and they made a big profit on the colonies after they inherited them. They lived an immoral life, releasing their colonial agents to exploit Penn's former commitments with the Indians. Their agents cheated them out of everything that William Penn had promised to them.

William Penn's family retained ownership of the colony of Pennsylvania until the American Revolution. At that time, the colony had grown to about 300,000 people. Between 1740 and 1776, Philadelphia presses alone published 11,000 pamphlets, almanacs, and books. And there were 7 newspapers. The city of Philadelphia was an intellectual center. The stage was set for American independence.

In 1984 President Ronald Reagan by an Act of Congress declared William Penn an Honorary Citizen of the United States.

NO CROSS, NO CROWN

William Penn's Preface

*M*Y FRIEND, WHY ARE you here on this earth?

There are just two main reasons:

1. to glorify God

2. to save your soul

That is heaven's decree, and it is as old as the earth itself. Unfortunately, people generally pay the least amount of attention to the most important things—we tend to major in minor priorities.

We don't want to think about these three things: (1) where we came from; (2) our duty to God; or (3) our original purpose. Instead, we choose to dedicate all of our time to ourselves; that is, whatever we think it takes to make us "happy." Our hearts are preoccupied with pride, greed, and the so-called "finer things of life." Did we create ourselves? No. We act as though this world only exists for us, as if we are not answerable to a Superior Power, namely, God.

How did we get into such a deplorable mind-set? The answer is plain. It was by our disobedience to the laws of God! In our hearts, we know what we should and shouldn't do, but as long as this inner disease (sin) plagues us, our attitudes will remain stubborn. We view God as our Enemy. And we don't think that He really loves us or that we truly need the "salvation" that His Son Jesus came to this world to offer us.

Dear reader, are *you* in that state of mind? If so, my advice to you is to get away somewhere by yourself and really think about this. Take a good, hard look at the condition of your soul. Christ has provided you the light to do this (John 1:9). Search your conscience very carefully. Be thorough. This is your life that we're talking about. Your eternal soul is at stake (Matt. 16:25)! You may only get one more chance to do this. If you blow it, you might never recover. There isn't enough money in the whole world to buy back that last opportunity of getting your head straight (Matt. 16:26).

Should you risk losing your soul and eternal salvation over this fleeting existence called earth? God is patient (2 Pet. 3:9), but even His patience has a limit. You must not provoke God (1 Cor. 10:22; Heb. 3:15-16). Do you want Him to reject you? Do you understand what that would mean (Heb. 10:31)!? You'd be damning yourself to an eternal hell (Matt. 5:22,29,30; 10:28; 18:9; Mark 9:43,45,47; 12:5; 16:23; 2 Pet. 2:4; Rev. 20:13-14)! Believe me, I know something about the terrors of the Lord, and I would try to persuade you to get serious about your own salvation (2 Cor. 5:10-11).

Yes, as one who is also well acquainted with the comfort, peace, joy, and pleasure of the ways of righteousness, I urge you to embrace the warnings of Christ's light and Spirit in your own conscience. Face up to the judgment of your sin! The fire burns only the stubble, and the wind blows only the chaff. If you will yield your whole self to Christ (body, soul, and spirit, 2 Cor. 7:1), he will "make all things new" (Rev. 21:5) for you— a new love, a new joy, a new peace, new deeds, a brand new way of living (2 Cor. 5:17), and, at the end, "a new heaven and a new earth" (Rev. 21:1).

People are like metals which still have impurities within them. They have sin mixed into the fabric of their lives. To become pure, both people and metals will have to go through an intense fire (1 Pet. 1:7) to get rid of those things that don't belong there. That's what the salvation process is all about. It's a purging (2 Pet. 1:9). So, the Word of God has been compared to a fire (Jer. 5:14; 20:9; 23:29), and the day of salvation is like an oven (Deut. 4:20), and Christ himself is similar to a refiner of silver (Matt. 3:12; 1 Cor. 3:12-13).

Come listen to me for a while. I just want what's best for you. (That is my only "plot." You must forgive me!)

Christ (the Refiner) has come near you. His grace has appeared to you (Titus 2:11). It shows you the lusts of the world, and it teaches you to deny them (Titus 2:12). Receive his instruction, and this will change you. The medicine of the Great Physician will cure you (Matt. 9:12; Mark 2:17; Luke 5:31). He is as infallible as he is free. He comes to you without money but with certainty. A touch of his garment brought healing long ago (Matt. 9:20; 14:36), and he can do it again today. His power is still the same (Heb. 13:8). It cannot be exhausted, because the totality of divinity lives embodied in Christ (Col. 2:9). Praise God for His sufficiency (2 Cor. 3:5)! God empowered Christ with all the might needed to save all those who come to God through Christ. If you'll respond, he *will* change you. Your vile body will become like his glorious body (Philp. 3:21). He is the great philosopher indeed—the Wisdom of God (1 Cor. 1:24) who turns lead into gold, and vile things into precious things. He alone can make saints out of sinners, and almost gods of men!

Therefore, what must we do in order to witness his power and love? This is the crown, but where is the cross? Where is the bitter cup and the bloody baptism (Matt. 20:22-23)? Come, be like him, because this transcendent joy will lift up your head above the world. Then your salvation will draw near indeed (Luke 21:28).

Christ's cross is Christ's way to Christ's crown. This is the subject of the following book. It was first written during my confinement in the Tower of London in 1668. And now it has been reprinted with additional thoughts and testimonies, so that you, dear reader, may be won to Christ. And, if you are already won, then you can be brought even nearer to him. God in His everlasting kindness has guided my feet onto this path in the flower of my youth. I was only 22 years old. Then He took me by the hand and led me out of the pleasures, vanities, and hopes of this world. I have tasted of Christ's judgments and mercies, as well as tasted of the world's frowns and reproaches. Nevertheless, I rejoice in my experiences, and I dedicate them all to your service in Christ. This book has been anticipated for several years. It is a debt that I have owed for a long time. I have now paid that debt and delivered my soul. I leave it now to my country and to the world of Christians. May my God make this an effective tool for them all. May this book turn their hearts away from that envy, hatred, and bitterness which they might have against one another concerning worldly things. May it turn them away from sacrificing humanity and love, away from selfish ambition and greed, for which they fill the earth with trouble and oppression. In receiving the Spirit of Christ into their hearts, may they yield the fruits of love, peace, joy, self-control, patience, and brotherly kindness (Gal. 5:22; 2 Pet. 1:7). May they, in body, soul, and spirit, make a triple league against the world, the flesh, and the Devil, who are the common enemies of mankind. And, having conquered those things through a life of self-denial, by the power of the cross of Jesus, may they finally reach the eternal rest and kingdom of God.

I so desire, and so I pray.

Your fervent Christian friend,

WILLIAM PENN
Worminghurst in Sussex
June 1, 1682

CHAPTER 1

What it Takes to be a Real Christian

WHAT SHOULD BE OF the greatest importance to everyone? My answer: Knowing all about the New Testament teaching concerning the cross of Christ. But that's not enough—we must also obey that doctrine! Since ancient times, that is the only door to true Christianity, the only path to true happiness.

Unfortunately, I'm very sad to say, the meaning of the cross of Christ is so poorly understood and so neglected by professing "Christians" today that they cannot seem to fathom what Jesus actually said in the first century in these two passages: "The person who does not carry his own cross cannot be my follower" (Luke 14:27). And, "If anyone wants to follow me, he must carry his cross every day. He must say no to himself and follow me" (Luke 9:23). This clear-cut lesson of Christ is bitterly contradicted by the current vanity, superstition, and excesses of so-called "Christians." They are generally deceiving themselves into thinking that they are actually following Christ and that they will ultimately be saved eternally.

DEGENERATE "CHRISTIANITY"

WE MIGHT POLITELY LIKE to call certain countries "Christian nations," but, to be completely accurate, we must admit that very little of true Christianity has endured. Those nations are "Christian" in name only! This is true despite all the tremendous advantages that they have received from the divine truth of the Holy Bible which depicts the life of Christ, his teachings, his miracles, his death, his resurrection, and his ascension to the right hand of God, along with the gifts of his Holy Spirit. In addition, the writings, the deeds, and the martyrdoms of Jesus' dear followers down through history have largely been forgotten. So, what's left of true "Christianity"? Very little indeed. Pagan ways have simply taken over. So-called "Christians" are just heathens in disguise!

Technically speaking, they may not worship the same idols as the pagans, but they approach the worship of Christ with the same attitude. How can they do otherwise as long as they are guided by the same worldly passions? The unconverted "Christian" and the pagan man really have the same religion. Although they both have different objects toward which they direct their prayers, that so-called "adoration" is merely ritualistic. The deity which they are actually worshiping is Satan, "the god of this world" (2 Cor. 4:4). He is the great lord of lusts. And, with their whole powers of soul and sense, they are actually bowing down to the Devil. They keep on asking the same old secular questions: "Where is our next meal coming from?" "How can we afford new clothes?" "What about our entertainment?" "How do we get rich and powerful?" "How can I become famous?" "Where are we going to acquire enough land for our children to inherit?" Jesus answers all these questions with Matt. 6:31-34: "So, don't worry, thinking to yourself, 'What will we eat?' or, 'What will we drink?' or, 'What will we wear?' People without God put all these things first. Your heavenly Father knows you need all these things. So, put first

God's kingdom and what is right. Then all the things you need will be given to you. Don't worry about tomorrow, because tomorrow will have its own worries. There is enough trouble in just one day."

The banal sensuality of this world is most pathetically expressed by the beloved Apostle John in these words: "These are the evil things in the world: (1) wanting sinful things to please our bodies; (2) wanting the things that we see; and, (3) being too proud of the things that we have. None of those things come from the Father; each one of them comes from the world." (1 John 2:16). According to Col. 3:5, all sin must be killed outright!

Of what does wretched "Christendom" consist? If one honestly reflects upon this question and doesn't try to deny it, sad to say, *worldly* desires dominate the thoughts and lives of so many so-called "Christians." And it's getting worse and worse as time goes on. In fact, people seem to be improving on new ways to sin! Instead of advancing virtue, they have scandalously fallen below the lifestyle of heathens. Rampant is sexual excess, indecency, impurity, drunkenness, profanity, lying, slander, treachery, conceit, jealousy, cruelty, greed, injustice, and oppression. Such things are now commonplace, even among so-called "committed Christians!" This has caused many unbelievers to scorn our holy religion. Setting a good example would have won infidels over to Christ, but instead they are being driven away! Good people are supposed to be "the salt of the earth," preserving the best ideals of society. As far as influence is concerned, Mark 9:50 states, "Salt is a good thing, but if the salt loses its salty taste, then it is no good. You cannot make it salty again."

JESUS' OWN PEOPLE DID NOT ACCEPT HIM

CHRISTIANITY WAS ONCE GLORIOUS, and those who professed it were pure. That was before the defection occurred early on (Acts 20:29-30). Look how badly the Jews treated the blessed Savior of mankind. How tragic! Because of their ignorance (Acts 3:17) and extreme prejudice against his divine appearance, they refused to acknowledge him when he came (John 1:11). Instead, they persecuted him for three years and finally crucified him one day.

But the cruelty of the false Christians lasts longer. Along with Judas Iscariot, they claim to believe in the Savior but then they betray him by a perpetual apostasy in the way they live, ignoring the self-denial and holiness of his teachings. The author of the Letter to the Hebrews tells us about them: "But they have fallen away. It is impossible to bring them back to a change of heart. In their lives, they nail the Son of God to the cross again, shaming him publicly" (Heb. 6:6). How do they do it? Their faith is a lie! The Apostle John describes their defiled hearts in the Book of Revelation in this manner: "Their dead bodies will lie exposed in the streets of the great city. (Spiritually, it is named Sodom and Egypt, where their Lord was nailed to the cross.) They won't allow their bodies to be buried" (Rev. 11:8-9a).

Long ago, Christ said, "The enemies of a person might be the members of his own family" (Matt. 10:36). In the same way, Christ's enemies are chiefly now those who claim to believe in his name. They are the actually ones who spit on him, who crown him with thorns, who pierce him, and who give him vinegar to drink (Matt. 27:30-35)!

This is not hard to comprehend because they live by the same evil nature and principles that the Jews did. The Jews crucified him outwardly, but so-called "Christians" today crucify him inwardly. They now reject the grace of God in their own hearts. So, they are related to the hard-hearted Jews who resisted the grace of God which appeared in and through Christ!

Sin is the same the world over. A liar may not be a drunkard, but they're both sinners. It doesn't make any difference whether you are a murderer, a foul-mouthed person, or a sexual sinner, you are all in the same boat. All branches from this wicked root are related to one another. All these people have only one father, the Devil (John 8:44). Christ said to the professing Jews of the visible "church" of that era: "If you were Abraham's children, you would be doing the things that Abraham did. Abraham would not have done this, but now you are trying to kill me. I have told you the truth which I heard when I was with God!" (John 8:39-40). The Lord Jesus told them plainly: "I am telling you the truth: Every person who continues to sin is a slave of sin" (John 8:34). Those people were doing the Devil's work. Therefore, they were the Devil's children (Acts 13:10; 1 John 3:10)!

Jesus' point is still valid. Paul said the same thing in his letter to the Roman Christians: "Surely you know that you are slaves to whomever you offer yourselves to obey? The one you obey is your master" (Rom. 6:16). Similarly, the Apostle John wrote to the ancient church: "Little children, don't let anyone fool you. . . . The person who continues to sin belongs to the Devil" (1 John 3:7-8). In the Garden of Gethsemane, was Judas Iscariot a better man because he said, "Greetings, Rabbi" and then kissed him (Matt. 26:49)? By no means! His greeting was only a signal of his treachery, a token by which the bloodthirsty Jews could know exactly which one Jesus was and therefore to arrest him. Judas called Jesus "Rabbi" (which means "great one"), but Judas betrayed him (see Luke 6:46). Judas kissed him, but he sold him out. The same is true of a false Christian religion. It's just lip-service!

If many of today's so-called "Christians" are asked, "Is Christ your Lord?" They always answer, "Of course, he is our Lord." Very well, but do you keep his commandments!? (See John 14:15). They reply, "No." How then are you his followers!? But they respond, "But it's impossible to keep his commandments! No one can keep them all!" Are you saying that it is impossible to be a true Christian? Is Christ being unreasonable? Does he reap where he has not sown (Gal. 6:7-8)? Is he asking something of us that he hasn't given us the power to do? Are we like Judas, ready to sell out Jesus in order to gratify the passions that we want to indulge in the most? Long ago, God said to the self-righteous Jews that they tried to make God serve their sins as well as for their sins (Isa. 43:24).

A WOLF IS NOT A LAMB

A WOLF IS NOT a sheep, and a vulture is not a dove. Let no one deceive himself about the two very different types of people. Jesus said, "They can be recognized by the things they produce. Do people get grapes from thorn bushes? No. Do they gather figs from thorny weeds? No." (Matt. 7:16). It doesn't matter what church or social class you belong to or what form of religion you practice. If you *deny* the power of God's truth to mankind, then you only have "a form of godliness" (2 Tim. 3:5). You are just saying "yes" to the outer form of religion, but you are saying "no" to its inner power. You're unconverted! You are a member of a false church!

This fake church may call herself "the bride of the Lamb" (Rev. 21:2; 22:17), or, "the church of Christ," but she is actually that mysterious "Babylon the Great" who is properly called "the mother of whores and the filthy things of the world" (Rev. 17:5). This is a valid comparison because this counterfeit church has degenerated from Christian purity and plunged herself headlong into all the same sorts of things that once existed in pagan, ancient Babylon. The word "Babylon" in the Book of Revelation is symbolic of any worldly domain whose secular pride and luxury know no bounds. As she was then, so mystical "Babylon" is now. This hypocritical church is the great enemy of God's true people!

It is true that those who are "born of the spirit" (John 3:5,6,8), those who have been truly circumcised in their hearts (Deut. 10:16; 30:6; Jer. 4:4; Rom. 2:29), are hated and persecuted by those who are "born of the flesh" (John 3:6; Gal. 4:29). True Christians are persecuted by the apostate church of false Christians. This perverted church tries to make everyone conform to her vain traditions (Matt. 15:1-9), methods, doctrines, worship, dress code, and speech. It's bad enough that she has departed from ancient purity (1 Tim. 4:1-3), she forces others to do so too. She gives no rest to those who will not partake with her in that same degeneracy or to receive her official "mark" (Rev. 13:16-17; 14:9,11; 15:2; 16:2; 19:20; 20:4). Are we any wiser than her, the mother church?[1] No, nor can anyone make war with "the beast" that she rides upon (Rev. 17:3,7), those worldly powers that protect her (Rev. 17:12) and who vow to support her against the cries of her dissenters (Rev. 17:13). All must either conform or perish!

Therefore, the slain witnesses and the blood of the souls under the altar (Rev. 6:9) are found within the walls of this mystical "Babylon," this great city of false Christians. These things are charged against her by the Holy Spirit in the Book of Revelation. It is not strange that "Babylon" would slay the servants of their crucified Lord? It is ironic and barbarous that she would kill her own Husband (that is, Christ, Rev. 21:2) and murder her own Savior!

Since the early days, several generations have continued to disobey the truth. And, the divine light of their souls has been extinguished in the dominion of darkness. They forgot what man once was, or what man should be now. They prided themselves upon professing true "Christianity," but they wouldn't know pure Christianity if they ever saw it. Their beliefs about salvation are so carnal and false that they call good "evil" and evil "good." They make a devil a Christian, and a saint a devil. They are deceived into thinking that they are the children of God while they remain in a state of disobedience to His holy commandments. They think they are disciples of Jesus, even though they rebel against his cross. They pretend to be members of his true church which is "without spot or wrinkle," (Eph. 5:27) even though their lives are full of spots and wrinkles (2 Pet. 2:13; Jude 1: 12). They are truly self-deceived! They are "at peace" in their sins (Jer. 6:14; 8:11), and they feel secure in their transgressions (Isa. 50:1; 59:2-15). Their vain hope silences their "convictions" and overlays all tender inclinations toward repentance. They mistake their so-called "duty to God" as being genuine when they are actually rebelling against Him!

They are walking on the edge of a dangerous cliff, and they are

1 the Roman Catholic Church

flattering themselves until they die. Then the judgments of the one true God will "wake them up" (Rom. 13:11) from their spiritual lethargy. They will find out soon enough that their evil lives were lived in vain! Along with the anguish of the wicked, they will receive the "reward" of their work (Matt. 25:30-33,41,46). This has always been (and will always be) the doom of all worldly Christians!

AN INVITATION TO PICK UP THE DAILY CROSS

I'M WELL ACQUAINTED WITH "the terror of the Lord" (2 Cor. 5:11), and I'm trying to "work out my own salvation" (Philp. 2:12). But, compassion alone is enough to cause me to speak out against this world's superstitions and lusts. I invite those who merely claim to be "Christian" to simply take up the cross every day (Luke 9:23). The knowledge and obedience of the daily cross of Christ is the *only* way to be truly happy as a real Christian and as a devoted follower of Christ. Christ gave us "the Way" (John 14:6; Acts 9:2; 16:17; 18:26; 19:9,23; 22:4; 24:14,22) in order to bless us and bring us into "a newness of life" (Rom. 6:4). Instead, fake Christians usurp the name of "Christian" (Acts 11:26; 26:28; 1 Pet. 4:16). They are now spiritually dead (Eph. 2:1; Col. 2:13), instead of being "dead to the world" (Rom. 6:6; Gal. 2:19-20; 5:24; 6:14; Eph. 4:22; Col. 3:5,9,10) by the power of the cross. He has made us true partakers of his resurrection (Rom. 6:5; Philp. 3:10).

Those who are truly "in Christ" (Rom. 6:3-4; 8:1; 12:5; Gal. 3:26-27) that is, redeemed by Christ, and intensely interested in him, are "*new* creatures" (2 Cor. 5:17; Gal. 6:15). They have received a *new* will; it is not their own will but the will of God. They truly pray, and they do not mock God when they say: "Thy will be done on earth as it is in heaven" (Matt. 6:10). They have *new* affections, set on the things above, not upon things of this earth (Col. 3:1-2). They make Christ their eternal treasure (Matt. 13:44,52; 2 Cor. 4:7; 6:10; Eph. 3:8; Col. 1:27; 2:3). Theirs is a *new* faith (Rom. 5:1;

1 John 5:4), the kind that overcomes the snares and temptations of the world's spirit in them or in others (John 16:33; Rom. 12:21; 1 John 2:13-14; 4:4; 5:4-5; Rev. 2:7,11,17,26; 3:5,12,21; 21:7). Lastly, they'll perform *new* deeds, not of a superstitious contrivance or of human invention, but the pure "fruits of the Spirit" (Gal. 5:22; Eph. 5:9) working in them, such as love, joy, peace, meekness, long-suffering, self-control, brotherly kindness, faith, patience, gentleness, and goodness, against which there is no law (Gal. 5:23).

Some do not have the Spirit of Christ in them—they do not walk in Christ (1 John 1:6-7; 2:6; 2 John 26; 3 John 1:4). The Apostle Paul has told us that such a person does not belong to Christ (Rom. 8:9). Instead, the wrath of God and condemnation of the law rests upon them (Rom. 1:18; 2:5,8; 5:9; Eph. 2:3; 5:6; Col. 3:6; 1 Thess. 1:10; 2:16; 5:9; Rev. 6:16). For since "there is no condemnation to those who are in Christ Jesus" (Rom. 8:1), "who walk not after the flesh but after the Spirit" (Rom. 8:4), which is what Paul taught in his letter to the Christians living in Rome. Therefore, those who do *not* live according to the Holy Spirit—by the Apostle Paul's doctrine—are *not* "in Christ." These sinners have no interest in Christ nor do they have a just assertion for being saved by Christ. Consequently, there *is* condemnation for such people!

EVIL PEOPLE CONDEMN THEMSELVES

THE TRUTH IS THE religion of the wicked is a lie! The prophet Isaiah said: " 'There is no peace for evil people.' says Yahweh" (Isaiah 48:22). Indeed there can be no peace at all. They are rebuked by their own consciences and condemned in their own hearts because of their disobedience. Wherever they go, disapproval will go with them. Trouble often haunts them everywhere. God is offended; He pricks them. By His light, in their presence, He sets their sins in order. Sometimes they strive to appease Him by their man-made devotion and so-called "worship." But it is in vain because the true worship of God is doing His will (Rom. 12:1-3), which they are transgressing. The rest is only a false compliment, like the one who said to his father that he would go but he did not go (Matt. 21:29-31). Sometimes they rush to various sporting events with like-minded "fans" to drown out the voice of their conscience. They want to blunt its accusing arrows, to chase away any troubling thoughts, to put themselves out of the reach of the disquieter of their pleasures. Nevertheless, Almighty God will surely overtake them. For those who reject the terms of His mercy there is no escape from His final justice. Impenitent rebels to His law might call out to the mountains, and run to the caves of the earth for protection (Rev. 6:15), but it will all be in vain! His all-searching eye will penetrate even their thickest coverings and will illuminate that obscurity. It will terrify their guilty souls; they'll never be able to extinguish that penetrating shaft of light! Indeed, their Accuser is with them. They can no more be rid of Him than they could run away from themselves. He'll be in the midst of them; He'll stick close to them. That spirit which bears witness with the spirits of the righteous will bear witness against their spirits. Yes, the Apostle John, says that their own hearts will abundantly come in against them testifying: "And when our conscience makes us feel guilty, we still may have peace before God, because God is greater than our conscience. God knows everything" (1 John 3:19-20).

So, there is no escaping the judgments of God. His power is infinite. On that Day of Judgment, arrogant and prosperous "Christians" will learn that "God is no respecter of persons" (Acts 10:34). God treats everyone the same. All "sects" and "denominations" will be swallowed up in either one of two categories. There are just two kinds of people: sheep or goats (Matt. 25:31-33), the good people or the bad people, and the just or the unjust (Acts 24:15). Even the very righteous people will be put on trial. A holy man once cried out with these words: "The Scripture says: 'If a good man will barely be saved, then where will the ungodly sinner be!?' (Prov. 11:31) Listen, good people will be rewarded on earth. And, an evil, sinful person will surely be punished!" (1 Pet. 4:18). Since their thoughts, words,

and works must stand the test, and come under scrutiny before the impartial Judge of heaven and earth, how then will the ungodly be exempted?
No, we are told by Him who cannot lie (Titus 1:2) that many will exclaim,
"Lord, Lord!" (Matt. 7:21) setting forth their claims of religiosity and re-
counting the pious works that they have done in his name (Matt. 7:22)
in order to get on God's good side, but they will still be rejected with
these piercing words, "You people who are doing wrong, go away from
me, because I never knew you!" (Matt. 7:23). As if Jesus said, "Get out of
here, you evil-doers! Though you alleged to know me, I do not know
you! Your vain and evil lies have made you unfit for my holy kingdom. Go
away! Go to the gods whom you have served, your beloved 'lusts' that you
worshiped, and the evil world that you coveted so much and adored. Let
those gods save you now—if they can—from the wrath which will surely
come upon you. You will be paid back for the deeds you have done" (Rom.
6:23). Here is the result of all their work that was built upon the sand (Matt.
7:26). The breath of the Judge will blow it down (Matt. 7:27), and how terrible will be its collapse! The righteous people are so much better off than
the wicked. Moses wrote: "Let me die like good people do. Let me end
up like them!" (Num. 23:10). Jesus (the Judge) smiles as he casts his loving eye upon his own sheep when he invites them to him: " 'Come, take
what belongs to you—the kingdom which was prepared for you since the
beginning of the world.' (Matt. 25:34). 'Eternal life will go to those who,
by patiently doing good things, are looking for glory, honor, and life with
no end' (Rom. 2:7). You have been the true companions of my tribula-
tion (Rev. 7:14) and cross, and, with unwearied faithfulness (Rev. 2:10,13;
17:14), in obedience to my holy will (Rev. 3:8,10; 12:17; 14:12; 22:7,9),
valiantly endured to the end (Rev. 1:9; 2:3,19; 13:10; 14:12), looking to
me, the Author of your precious faith (Heb. 12:2), for the recompense of
reward that I have promised to them (Rev. 22:12) who love me (2 Tim.
4:8), and who faint not (Luke 18:1; 2 Cor. 4:16; Gal. 6:9). O enter ye 'into
the joy of your Lord' (Matt. 25:23), and 'inherit the kingdom prepared for
you from the foundation of the world' " (Matt. 25:34).

A PRAYER FOR "CHRISTENDOM"

O Christendom, I pray most fervently, after all of your lofty claims on behalf of Christ and his meek and holy religion, that your unchristian ways will not cast you adrift in the world and cause you to lose your "great salvation" (Heb. 2:3) in the end. Hear me, I beg you! Can Christ be your Lord and yet you won't obey him!? Or, can you be his servant but never serve him!? No! "Don't be fooled! You cannot mock God. A person harvests only the things that he plants." (Gal. 6:7). He is *not* your Savior as long as you reject his mercy in your heart. He saves you by his grace (Eph. 2:8-9). What has he saved you from? Has he not saved you from your own sinful lusts, your worldly affections, and your vain lifestyle (1 John 2:16)? If you are still living by those things, then he is not your Savior at all! For, though he has been offered as a Savior to everyone, yet he is only a Savior to those who are actually saved by him. And, those who continue to practice those evils (by which they are lost from God) cannot be saved by him. He came to save them from those things (Luke 19:10).

Christ came to save mankind from sin, death, and punishment. Paul wrote: "The pay you get for sinning is death, but God's gift is eternal life in Christ Jesus, our Lord" (Rom. 6:23). Those who are not saved—delivered by the power of Christ in their souls, from the power that sin has has over them—can never be saved from death and God's anger as long as they *continue* to live in sin (1 John 3:6,9).

Look how far some people have gone to obtain victory over those evil dispositions and fleshly lusts that they were addicted to! These people have been truly saved from those sins. They are witnesses of the redemption that comes through Jesus Christ. The very name of "Jesus" showed his mission: "You will name him 'Jesus,' because he will save his people from their sins." (Matt. 1:21). John the Baptist said of Christ: "Look, God's Lamb who will take away the world's sin!" (John 1:29). This means: "Behold the

One whom God has given to enlighten people for salvation." This deliverance is available to all those who accept him (John 1:11-12). His light and his mercy is in their hearts. They must take up their daily cross and follow him (Luke 9:23). They must deny themselves the pleasure of satisfying their worldly desires. They must not sin against that certain knowledge. God has imparted His will; they know what they ought to do.

CHAPTER 2

Keep on Following Christ

*I*F YOU WILL RE-READ Chapter 1 carefully, you will greatly benefit. Everyone has the lamp of the Lord inside them (John 1:9), but you must use it. You *will* understand, unless your lamp is utterly extinct!

The following points are obvious:

First, how far have you fallen spiritually? Have you become like a cage full of "unclean birds" (Lev. 11:13-19; Deut. 14:12-18) in the temple of the Lord? Have you transformed the "house of prayer" (Isa. 56:7) into "a den of thieves" (Matt. 21:13; Mark 11:17; Luke 19:46), a "synagogue of Satan" (Rev. 2:9; 3:9), and a receptacle of every defiled spirit?

Second, along with the clear-cut, wholesale defection from Christ's Way, have you over-rated your own corrupt self? Have you been affected by nominal "Christianity"? Have you tragically deluded yourself by adopting a false hope of salvation?

Backsliding is a dangerous disease, but fantasy is almost incurable.

Nevertheless, God is merciful. He takes no delight in the eternal death of poor sinners (Ezek. 18:20,23,24). God is patient with us. "No, He wants everyone to find room for a change in their hearts. He doesn't

19

want anyone to be lost" (2 Pet. 3:9). He desires that everyone would come to the knowledge and obedience of the truth and be saved. He has sent His Son to be our Savior (Matt. 1:21). Jesus "is the way our sins are taken away—the way all people may have their sins taken away" (1 John 2:2). "Though the evil one is everywhere in the whole world, we know we belong to God" (1 John 5:19).

Those who believe in Jesus and follow him will feel the righteousness of God when their sins are forgiven, thereby blotting out their transgressions (Rom. 3:25; Heb. 9:24-28). This is the universal remedy. This medicine cures all diseases!

JESUS IS THE LIGHT OF THE WORLD

BUT YOU MAY ASK: Who is Christ? Where is he? How does one acquire and administer this mighty cure? I will tell you.

First, Jesus of Nazareth is the great spiritual "light of the world" (John 8:12) who enlightens everyone who comes into the world. By this light he shows them their dark deeds and rebukes them for committing them.

Second, he's not far away from you, as the Apostle Paul said of God to the Athenians (Acts 17:27). And, Christ himself said, "Listen, I stand at the door. I am knocking. If anyone hears my voice and opens the door, I will come inside with him. We will have dinner together" (Rev. 3:20). What "door" could this be? It is a person's heart.

NO ROOM IN THE INN

THAT INN AT OLD Bethlehem (Luke 2:7) was full of guests. But there was no room left for the Christ child. Instead, he was born in a stable with the animals. Where is *your* heart? Is it with those who are too busy to make room for the Savior or has his salvation come into your house (Luke

19:9)? Salvation might be at your doorstep. And you might claim that you possess it. But if Jesus calls you—if he is still knocking—will you answer him? If his light still shines, if it corrects you, then there may be hope that your day is not over and that repentance is not yet hidden from your eyes. Jesus still loves you; he's not going to give up on you!

So, O Christendom, you must believe, accept, and apply Jesus (the medicine) properly! This is absolutely necessary for your soul to live with him forever. He told the Jews: "I am going away and you will look for me, but you will die in your sins. You cannot come where I am going. I told you that you would die in your sins. If you don't believe that I am the one, you will die in your sins" (John 8:21,24). They did not receive him because they did not believe in him. Therefore, they did not benefit. But those who did believe in Jesus accepted him. The Scripture says: "But he gave the right to become God's children to those who did accept him, to those who believe in his name. They were born, not in a human way, from the natural human desire of men, but born of God" (John 1:12-13). They became children of God according to God's will and because they were made holy by His Spirit. They were not children of God after the fashions, prescriptions, and traditions of men (Matt. 15:9), who call themselves "his church" and "his people." No, it was not after the will of flesh and blood, and the invention of carnal man, unacquainted with the regeneration and power of the Holy Spirit, but children of God, according to His will and the working and sanctification of His Spirit and Word of Life in them!

Jesus is the means by which our sins are taken away (1 John 2:2). God "uses Christ to bring us back to Himself" (2 Cor. 5:18). Jesus came to find lost people and to save them (Luke 19:10). "With God's gracious love, we are made right with God through Christ Jesus who sets us free" (Rom. 3:24). "His blood has set us free. We have the forgiveness of sins!" (Eph. 1:7).

You will die in your sins (John 8:24) unless you truly believe in Jesus, the one who is standing at the door of your heart and knocking. He is exposing your sins to you, and he is asking you to change your life.

Where he has gone you won't be able to go (John 8:21). If you don't believe in him, it's impossible for him to do you any good. Christ does not work against faith but by it.

Long ago, this was written: "So, because they did not believe, Jesus did not perform many miracles there. Jesus was not able to perform a miracle there" (Matt. 13:58; Mark 6:5). If you truly believe in Jesus, then your ear will be attentive to his voice within you. You will open the door of your heart wide when he knocks. When you discover his light, you will yield to him. The teachings of his grace will become very dear to you.

WHAT IS TRUE FAITH?

WE SHOULD HAVE A holy respect for God. We should never offend God. We ought to have a deep reverence for His precepts. And, we need to be very sensitive to the inward testimony of His Spirit. In all ages, God's children have been safely led to glory by His Spirit. Those who truly believe in Christ in their souls receive an inward force and ability to do whatever Christ requires. They are strong enough to kill their selfish desires, to control their emotions, to resist evil influences, and to deny themselves. They can overcome the world's most enticing allurements. Such is a life which is patterned after the blessed cross of Christ.

Reader, if you intend to be a true disciple of Jesus, then you must adopt this kind of life. You cannot say that you believe in Christ and accept him while you are rejecting his cross! The acceptance of Christ is the means that God has ordained for salvation (John 14:6). So, carrying one's cross daily behind Jesus (Luke 9:23) is the only sure way of knowing that you have received him! Therefore, Jesus commands this as the true test of discipleship. He said: "If anyone wants to follow me, he must carry his cross and follow me. He must say no to himself" (Matt. 16:24).

O Christendom, isn't this what you've always wanted? Doesn't the lack of this commitment prove why you are so miserable in your departure from true Christianity? You should think deeply about this. It's your duty to do so. It's the only way you can be restored.

Just as a physician must know a great deal in order to diagnose any disease so that the proper medicine can be applied, so you must be enlightened about how you can recover. Then you will know and evaluate what caused your spiritual lapse and how you contracted the disease (sin) in the first place. To do this, you must have a general overview of your original condition. You ought to know how previous Christians lived the Christian life. Learn from their example.

THE MISSION OF THE APOSTLES

THE APOSTLES WERE TRYING to turn people "from darkness to light" (that is, from sin to righteousness), "turning from the power of Satan back to God. Then they can receive forgiveness of their sins. They will have a share with those people who have been made holy by trusting in Christ" (Acts 26:18). Instead of yielding to the temptations of Satan (the prince of darkness who wants to retain their souls in the service of sin), people should turn their minds toward Christ's reappearance. He is the Light and the Savior of the world. By his light, he shines in their souls and allows them to see their sins. He discovers every tendency in them toward evil and rebukes them when they succumb to it. Jesus does this so that people may become "children of light" (John 12:36; Eph. 5:8; 1 Thess. 5:5) and walk "in the paths of righteousness" (Psalms 23:3).

Christ endowed his apostles with his spirit and power for this blessed work of reformation. No longer would men sleep in the security of sin and the ignorance of God. Instead, they would wake up to righteousness so that the Lord Jesus could give them life. Christ gave them power so that they would quit sinning and deny themselves of the pleasures of wickedness. When they truly change their lives, they turn their hearts toward God by doing good things and thus find peace.

NO CROSS, NO CROWN

God truly blessed the ministry of those faithful apostles. They were his great ambassadors to mankind. In just a few years, several thousand people changed their lives. They had lived lawlessly without God in the world, without any sense or fear of Him, being captivated by their fleshly lusts. They had lived as strangers (Eph. 2:12,19) to the work of the Holy Spirit in their hearts. But later they were affected inwardly and made alive by the Word of Life. Those people were made aware of the coming and the power of the Lord Jesus Christ as Judge (John 5:30; 8:16) and Law-giver (Gal. 6:2) in their souls. "The hidden things of darkness" (1 Cor. 4:5) were brought to light and condemned by the holy light and spirit of Christ.

They sincerely repented of their "dead works" (Heb. 6:1; 9:14) and they were "born again" (John 3:5; 1 Pet. 1:23), so that they could serve the living God "in newness of spirit" (Rom. 7:6). From then on, they did not live for themselves. Neither were they carried away by those former sinful desires. But "the law of the Spirit of life in Christ" (Rom. 8:2) was their delight. They meditated on this law day and night (Psalms 1:2). Their respect for God was no longer taught by the precepts of men (Isa. 29:13), but from the knowledge which they had received by God's own handiwork and impressions upon their souls. They had quit their old masters—the world, the flesh, and the Devil. And they surrendered themselves to the holy guidance of the grace of Christ who taught them to restrict themselves voluntarily. The Apostle Paul wrote: "The gracious love of God has appeared to save all mankind. It trains us to say no to ungodly ways and worldly desires and to live self-controlled, upright, and godly lives in this world" (Titus 2:11-12).

This was indeed the cross of Christ. Picking up the cross and carrying it was what gave them victory. By this cross they died daily to the old life that they had lived before. By a holy watchfulness against the secret inclinations of evil in their hearts they crushed sin before it could get started. "The evil one cannot touch him" (1 John 5:18).

Christ enlightened them, and this light uncovered all of Satan's attacks upon their minds. The power which they received through their inward obedience to that blessed light enabled them to vanquish Satan and all of his stratagems. Where once nothing was examined, now nothing went un-examined (Acts 17:11). Every thought must come under scrutiny (2 Cor. 10:5). Each idea had to be approved before it was allowed any room in their minds. Fraternizing with the friends of the enemy was not tolerated. A strict guard was stationed at the very doorway of the soul.

Now the old heavens and earth (Rev. 21:1b), that is, the old way of living, that old carnal, shadowy, Jewish worship (Col. 2:16-17; Heb. 8:5; 10:1), have quickly passed away. All things have become new every day. There is an external Jew, but there is also an internal "Jew" whose circum-cision is of the heart, whose praise is not of man, but of God. It is in the spirit, not the letter (Rom. 2:28-29; 7:6; 2 Cor. 3:6).

THE GLORY OF THE CROSS

THE GLORY OF THE cross shine conspicuously through the self-denial of the lives of those who carried the cross daily. This struck the pagan peo-ple with astonishment. In a relatively short time it shook their altars, and discredited their oracles, and shocked the masses, and invaded the courts, and overcame their armies. The glory of the cross triumphantly led priests, magistrates, and generals behind it.

The early Christians had integrity. Their presence was powerful. God's power, which was with them, was invincible. It quenched fire. It daunted lions. It turned the edge of the sword away. It dulled the instruments of cruelty. It convicted judges and converted executioners (Heb. 11:32-40; Isa. 43:2; Dan. 3:12-30).

Finally, no matter how their enemies tried to destroy them, it only in-creased their numbers. Their persecutors tried everything they could think of to extinguish the truth, but they ended up being great promoters of the truth (like Paul in Acts 9 or Darius in Dan. 6:16-28). The deep wisdom of God caused this. No vain thought or idle word or unseemly action was permitted among the early Christians. No, not an immodest look, no courtly dress, no festive apparel, no flattering talk or impressive titles—much less those lewd immoralities and scandalous vices now in vogue with so-called "Christians." Nothing of the latter sort was found among them. They didn't want to fritter away their precious time and waste it. Instead, they redeemed the time (Eph. 5:16; Col. 4:5) so that they would have enough time to work out their great salvation (Philp. 2:12a). They did this deliberately "with fear and trembling" (Philp. 2:12b), not with fancy dances and masquerade balls, by attending theaters, banquets, and casinos. No, no, they ensured that their heavenly calling and choice (2 Pet. 1:10) was more important to them than the trifling joys of mortality. Along with Moses, they saw the invisible. Go and find out that His loving-kindness is better than life. They sought the peace of His Spirit more than the favor of princes. They did not fear Caesar's wrath. Instead, they chose instead to sustain the sufferings of Christ as true pilgrims rather than to enjoy the pleasures of sin for just a little while. They regarded the reproaches against Christ to be of more value than the perishing treasures of the earth (Heb. 11:25-26). The tribulations of Christianity were more important than the comforts of this world, and the reproaches of one was superior to all the honor of the other. There was certainly no temptation in their persecutions that could shake their integrity.

THE DECLINE AND FALL OF "CHRISTIANITY"

BY THIS SHORT HISTORY, you can see what "Christendom" was, as well as what it is and what it ought to be. But, how did "Christendom" arise from something so meek, merciful, self-denying, suffering, temperate, holy, just, and good, so much like Christ, whose name she bore, to become so superstitious, idolatrous, persecuting, proud, passionate, envious, malicious, selfish, drunk, lascivious, unclean, lying, swearing, cursing, covetous, oppressing, cheating, as well as all the other abominations known on earth?

Undoubtedly, the reason of this degeneracy is an inward disregard for the light of Christ. It was always shining. It exposed the sins and rebuked them. It taught people and enabled them to resist sin. Light and grace revealed the most secret thoughts and searched the innermost parts, exposing sin. Not one unfruitful thought, word, or work of darkness was allowed to go unjudged. A fear toward God, and a holy abstinence from unrighteousness was at first not taught by the precepts of men. Once light and grace began to be set aside, that holy watch that was once set up, became careless. The restless enemy of man's good (Satan) quickly took advantage of this laxity with his temptations. His conquest was not difficult because he knew what was appealing to the inclinations of people.

NEGLECTING THE CROSS

WHAT ARE THE EFFECTS of not taking up Christ's holy yoke and bearing one's cross daily? If you are careless in your affections and do not keep a journal or check up on everything you do, you are indeed neglecting the cross. You must monitor your own conscience by Christ, your Light. Did your holy fear decay? Did your first love (Rev. 2:4) grow cold? Did your vanity abound and your duty become burdensome? Did formality come next instead of the power of godliness? Christ tried to draw the minds of his disciples away from an outward temple to the inward, spiritual worship of God. Unfortunately, a worldly, human, pompous worship was reintroduced and, a worldly priesthood, temple, and altar were re-established. The pure eye which repentance had opened grew dim. The "god of this world" (2 Cor. 4:4) reopened the eye of lust once more. Those worldly pleasures caused people to forget God. The luster of those allurements regained their old "beauty," resulting in a recommitment to a life that is completely secular.

Although there still remained the exterior forms of worship in

"Christendom," and a nominal and oral reverence to God and Christ, there was nothing of substance left. The "embarrassment" of Jesus' holy cross had ceased. The power of godliness was denied, and the concept of self-denial was lost. Although many clever ceremonies were invented, the blessed "fruits of the Spirit" were absent. A thousand shells cannot make one kernel; many corpses cannot make one living human being.

So, religion went downhill from experience to tradition, and true worship to meaningless form, from life to the letter. Instead of putting up lively and powerful requests to God animated by a deep sense of need for help from the Holy Spirit, a dull and insipid formality developed. It consists of certain bowings and cringing, ecclesiastical garments and furnishings, incense, soloists, and special music. All these things seem more suitable for the reception of some earthly prince than the heavenly worship of the one true and immortal God, who is an eternal, invisible Spirit (John 4:24).

Instead, hearts grew carnal and so did religion. They didn't like the way it was, so they shaped it according to their own liking, forgetting what the holy prophet had said: "Yahweh detests the worship that evil people offer. But He is very pleased with an honest person's prayer" (Prov. 15:8). James said, "And even if you do ask, you don't receive, because you ask, so that you may use it in an evil way for your own selfish desires" (James 4:3). This meant that they were asking with a heart that was not right. Are you insincere but unmortified? Since you are not asking with a faith that purifies the soul, you can never receive what is asked for. Therefore, someone could truly say that your condition is worsened by your religion. Although you are tempted to think that you are better off because of your religion, in fact, you are not.

Perhaps if you now understand your foul fall from primitive Christianity and that the true cause of this is the neglect of carrying the cross of Christ daily, then you might be able to teach yourself how to recover.

CHRIST'S INVITATION

LOOK, THE DOOR BY which you left is the same door you must use to come back in. In the same way, just as abandonment of the carrying of Jesus' cross daily has caused you to be lost, so picking up that cross again and enduring the daily cross will cause you to recover. Matthew 16:24 says: "If anyone wants to follow me, he must carry his cross and follow me. He must say no to himself." Luke 14:27 says, "The person who does not carry his own cross cannot be my follower." Nothing short of this total commitment will do! There will be no crown except by the cross! There is no eternal life unless one first dies to himself!

CHAPTER 3

Is It Your Cross?

O CHRISTENDOM, WHAT WAS MEANT by the "daily" cross (Luke 9:23) then, and what does it mean now? What is the doctrine of "the cross" in the New Testament? Here are the key questions which you must seriously consider:

1. What is the cross of Christ?
2. Where is the cross of Christ to be picked up?
3. How is the cross to be carried?
4. The cross crucifies sins, but what is entailed by that process?
5. And, what can be learned from notable, knowledgeable, pious Christians?

We must understand all of these things in order to get to heaven!

WHAT IS THE CROSS OF CHRIST?

THE CROSS OF CHRIST is symbolic. It was borrowed from a literal "tree" (see Acts 5:30; 10:39; 13:29; Gal. 3:13; and 1 Pet. 2:24). Christ submitted to the will of God (Matt. 26:42; Heb. 5:7-9; 10:7,9) on that physical cross, which was made of wood. Jesus suffered on it. Evil men killed him on it.

But the mystical "cross" is that divine grace and power which opposes the carnal wills of human beings. It contradicts their corrupt affections, and it constantly presents itself to the inordinate and fleshly appetites of their minds. Therefore, it may be correctly called "the instrument of man's utter death to the world." Whenever a person conforms to the will of God, that is a conscious submission to the implications of Jesus' cross. Nothing else can kill sin (Col. 3:5)! What else could account for our yielding to God, when, in the past, we didn't want to do it!?

In the early days, Paul (that famous and skillful apostle in spiritual things) rightly termed the preaching about the cross as "the power of God." To those who are perishing (then and now) the cross seems foolish: "To people who are being lost the message about Jesus' being nailed to a cross sounds silly, but it is God's power to us who are being saved" (1 Cor. 1:18). The lost were truly weary and heavily laden with sin (Matt. 11:28). Sin was burdensome and distasteful to them. They needed a Deliverer, but they didn't know it. The preaching of Jesus' cross became "the power of God" to believers. It was a proclamation of the divine power by which some of them became disciples of Christ and children of God. This Good News operated so powerfully upon them that no proud or licentious mockers could dissuade them from it, because they were in love with the cross of Christ. But to those who walked along the wide road which leads to destruction (Matt. 7:13) the preaching of the cross seemed ridiculous. Such persons dedicated all of their time and attention to the pleasures of their corrupt appetites in the full latitude of their lusts. Christ's yoke and bridle (Matt. 11:28-30) was intolerable to them.

WHERE IS THE CROSS?

WHERE IS THIS MYSTICAL "cross"? Was it only on Calvary's crown? And, from where must Jesus' cross be picked up?

The answer is simple: That cross is *within* us—it's in our heart and soul. The cross of Christ must be wherever sin is. Christ taught that all evil comes from inside us. Jesus said, "These things come from the inside of a man's heart: evil thoughts, sexual sin, stealing, murder, adultery, greed, all kinds of evil things, treachery, sensuality, jealousy, slander, bragging, foolishness. All these evil things come from the inside; they make a person unholy" (Mark 7:21-23).

So, the heart of man is the seat of sin. Wherever he is defiled, he must be made holy. And, wherever sin lives, there it must die. It must be crucified, that is, nailed to the cross of Christ! The Apostle Paul put it this way, "I stopped living for the law. I died to the law, so that I may now live for God. I[1] was killed on the cross with Christ. So, the life which I now live is not really me—it is Christ living in me! I still live in my body, but I live by faith in the Son of God. He is the one who loved me; he sacrificed himself for me" (Gal. 2:19-20). When evil seems "normal," it becomes natural for people to do wrong. The soul rules the body. When a corrupt nature sways the whole person, sin is coming from within.

Experience teaches every son and daughter of Adam that this principle is true. Satan's temptations are always directed at the mind, which is within. If one doesn't yield to a particular temptation, then his soul does not sin. But, if he embraces the suggestion, then something else happens: "After that desire has been conceived, it produces sin. Then the sin grows and results in death" (James 1:15). So, here is both the cause and the effect of transgressions—the very genesis of sin, its rise and result. In all of this, the heart of evil man is the Devil's factory, his workshop, and the place

---

1   literally, "my old life"

of his residence where he exercises his power and art. Therefore, the redemption of the soul is properly called the destruction of the works of the Devil (see 1 John 3:8). This is how everlasting righteousness is ushered in (Dan. 9:24). Some Jews once tried to defame Christ's miracle of casting out demons. They blasphemously attributed it to the so-called "power" of Beelzebul (that is, Satan) (Matt. 12:24). But Jesus asked them, "How can someone go into a strong man's house and take away his possessions? He must first tie up the strong man. Then he can rob the strong man's house" (Matt. 12:29). This only showed the contradiction that existed between Satan and his limited powers. It teaches us to recognize that the souls of the wicked ones are held in the Devil's domain. Also, all of Satan's evil deeds must first be "bound" by Christ. Christ destroys those sinful things and then takes possession of that house.[2] This makes it easy to know where the cross must be picked up. The strong man (the Devil) must first be controlled by Christ (the stronger man), and then Satan's stronghold will be plundered. After that, the Devil's temptations can be resisted within, that is, in the heart of man.

HOW DO I CARRY MY "CROSS" EVERY DAY? (LUKE 9:23)

SPIRITUALLY SPEAKING, JESUS' PHYSICAL cross had tremendous significance. The way of the cross (living the Christian life each day) is also spiritual. It is a consistent, inward submission of one's soul to the will of God. This yielding is manifested by the light of Christ within the consciences of people, even though such is contrary to their own inclinations. For example, when evil presents itself, we know we shouldn't yield to it, and God gives us the power to escape it (1 Cor. 10:13). However, after we've looked at the temptation for a while and gazed at it, we succumb to it, and are sometimes overcome by it. Guilt and condemnation ensue. But the cross

2   or, body

of Christ is that spirit and power within people which rebukes their fleshly lusts and affections. This message comes from God, not man.

So, picking up Jesus' cross is an entire resignation of one's soul to finding out what Jesus really wants from us. We are not consulting worldly pleasures, or carnal ease, or our own selfish interests. Such things are fleeting. Instead, we should continually be on guard against the very "appearance of evil" (1 Thess. 5:22). And, by the obedience of faith (Rom. 1:5; 16:26) to God, we ought to cheerfully sacrifice ourselves (Rom. 12:1) to Jesus' death on the cross. There's a little bit of Judas Iscariot in all of us! "Everyone has sinned and is far away from God's glory" (Rom. 3:23). In other words, in the heat of the siege, being impatient during the hour of our temptation, we have all betrayed Christ at one time or another, thus playing into the hands of Satan, the tempter (Matt. 4:3).

In real life, it is hard to be a true follower of Jesus. The way is narrow indeed, and the gate is very tight (Matt. 7:13). Not a single word or thought (2 Cor. 10:5) must be allowed to slip past the ever-present watchman (Matt. 24:42; 25:13; 26:38-41). We must always be circumspect (Acts 20:28; 1 Cor. 4:2; 1 Pet. 5:2,3,8), cautious, patient, and constant (1 Cor. 15:58). This is a holy "fear and trembling" (Philp. 2:12). This gives us an easy interpretation to that hard saying: "Flesh and blood cannot inherit the kingdom of God" (1 Cor. 15:50). That verse is referring to those who are captivated with fleshly lusts and affections. They cannot carry the cross, and they cannot endure the cross. So, they'll never get the crown. To reign, it is necessary first to suffer (Rom. 8:17) and then to endure (2 Tim. 2:12).

WHAT WAS THE PURPOSE OF THE CROSS?

WITH GOD'S HELP, I will now pursue this question, using the best knowledge that He has given to me through the experience of several years of following Jesus.

In man, the goal of the cross of Christ was self-denial. This world has an agenda that is the very opposite of that premise, namely, self-gratification. It's no wonder why the people of this world cannot understand the demands of Jesus' cross, much less be embraced by it. Nevertheless, the cross is the only true path. The Son of God has gone ahead of us. He knows the way. He drank that bitter cup. He was fully immersed in the pain. He has left us the example that we should "follow in his steps" (1 Pet. 2:21).

Matthew 20:20-23 says: "Then the mother of the sons of Zebedee, James and John, came to Jesus with her sons. She bowed down and asked him for something. Jesus said to her, 'What do you want?' She said to him, 'Promise me that these two sons of mine will sit on thrones in your kingdom, one at your right side and one at your left side.' Jesus answered them, 'You don't know what you are asking. Can you drink the cup of suffering which I am about to drink?' They said to Jesus, 'We are able.' Jesus said to them, 'Yes, you will drink from the cup of suffering which I will drink, but the privilege of sitting at my right side or my left side is not mine to give. Instead, those places belong to those for whom my Father prepared them.' "

The wife of Zebedee and her two sons put a hard question to Jesus. She wanted the very best for her sons, James and John—that one might sit at his right and the other at his left hand in Jesus' kingdom. But Jesus responded with this counter question: "Are ye able to drink of the cup that I shall drink of, and to be baptized with the baptism I am baptized with?" It seems that their faith was strong. They answered, "We are able." Upon which He replied, "Ye shall indeed drink of my cup, and be baptized with the baptism I am baptized with." But Jesus left their reward to his Father.

What was that "cup" that Jesus drank? And what was that immersion that he endured? In both cases, it was the denial of himself and the offering up of himself to the will of God by the eternal Spirit. He underwent the tribulations of his life and the agonies of his death upon the cross, all for the sake of man's salvation.

HAVE *YOU* SUFFERED FOR THE CROSS?

WHAT IS *OUR* CUP that we should drink? What is *our* cross that we must endure? It is the denial of ourselves, and not mere things to ourselves. Like Jesus, we must sacrifice ourselves by the same Spirit, doing the will of God for His service and suffering for His glory. That is true living. That is what obedience to the cross of Jesus really means.

This path is still "narrow" (Matt. 7:13-14). Before Christ came, that road was an uncharted way. At one time, there was no one to help, none worthy enough to open the seals (Rev. 5:2,5,9), to give us spiritual knowledge, to direct the course of mankind's recovery. But now Christ has come in the greatness of his love and strength. Though clothed with the infirmities of a mortal man (Heb. 2:9), being fortified within by the omnipotence of an immortal God (Matt. 26:53), Jesus traveled through all the perils and difficulties of humanity. He was the first to show us the unwalked path to true happiness.

Come, let us follow him! He is the tireless, victorious "Captain of our salvation" (Heb. 2:10). Neither Alexander the Great nor any of the mighty Caesars can compare to Jesus Christ! True, they were all great princes and conquerors. However, they operated on very different principles. Christ wasn't trying to become famous (John 7:4); his mission was to save mankind (Mark 9:9; Luke 19:10). On the other hand, those men ruined multitudes of people in order to augment their kingdoms. They vanquished others, but they could not control themselves. Christ conquered "self," and that is a far greater accomplishment. And, as far as merit is concerned, Christ is the most excellent "Prince of life" (Acts 3:15) and Conqueror (Rev. 6:2). Those secular generals advanced their empires through plunder and by blood, but Christ advanced his kingdom (John 18:36) through persuasion and suffering. Their prevailing method was always by force, but his conquest was never by compulsion. Misery and slavery followed all their victories, but Jesus brought greater freedom and happiness to all those whom he overcame. In everything that those despots did, they sought to please themselves, but in all that Jesus did, he only aimed to please his heavenly Father (John 5:30). So, who is "the King of kings and Lord of lords"? It is Jesus Christ (1 Tim. 6:15; Rev. 17:14; 19:16).

It is this most perfect pattern of self-denial that we too must follow. If we are ever to arrive in heaven, we'll have to truly understand the full meaning of what Jesus taught us about self-denial.

THE MEANING OF "SELF"

THERE IS A LAWFUL "self," and there is an unlawful "self." Both kinds of "self" must be denied for the sake of Jesus! Christ submitted totally to the will of God. He did not regard anything on this earth as precious; he only came to save us.

Everyone understands what the unlawful "self" is, because people everywhere greedily pursue that course every day. So, there's little need to explain that type of "self."

However, the lawful "self" (which we are to deny) consists of such things as: good fortune, ease, enjoyment, and abundance. These things are not in and of themselves evil. They are the bounty and blessings of God to us. It could be our husband, our wife, our children, our home, our land, our reputation, our liberty, or even life itself. These are all God's gifts to us which we may rightfully enjoy with pleasure. There's nothing wrong with these things. But, whenever God requires them of us, at whatever time the Lender calls for them, or He is pleased to test our affections by asking us to give them up, then nothing must be held back from God, the true Owner. When anything competes with God, then that thing must not be preferred. It *must* be surrendered. Christ himself descended from the glory of his Father (John 17:5), and he willingly made himself of no reputation among men. Though he was equal with God (John 5:18), he humbled himself, becoming like a servant. Yes, he suffered even the ignominious death of the cross. The Apostle Paul expressed it this way: "Do nothing from selfish ambition or conceited pride. Instead, humbly treat others better than yourselves. Look for what is important to others, not just what is important to you. Have the same attitude among you that Christ Jesus had: Though Christ was divine by nature, He did not think that being equal with God was something to hold onto. Instead, he emptied himself, taking on the very nature of a slave. He became like human beings, appearing in human form. He humbled himself. He obeyed, though it meant dying, even dying on a cross! So, God made him the most important. God gave him a name that is above every name" (Philp. 2:3-9).

This is the doctrine that Jesus teaches us: "The person who loves his father or mother more than me is not worthy of me. The person who loves his son or daughter more than me is not worthy of me" (Matt. 10:37). Again, "You must give everything you have. If you don't, you cannot be my follower!" (Luke 14:33). And, Jesus plainly told the young rich man that if he would ever attain eternal life, then he needed to sell everything and to follow Christ (Mark 10:21-22). That was a sad doctrine to that man. Like him, however, it is just as sad to those who, for all of their high pretences of religion, they truly love their possessions *more* than they love Christ! Nevertheless, this teaching about self-denial is the condition of eternal happiness. Jesus taught: "If anyone wants to follow me, he must carry his cross and follow me. He must say no to himself" (Matt. 16:24).

This doctrine of Christ made those honest fishermen quit their lawful trades in order to follow him (Matt. 4:18-20). When Jesus called them, they responded whole-heartedly. Others who were "waiting for the consolation of Israel" (Luke 2:25) offered up their estates (Acts 2:45; 4:34,37), their reputations (John 7:50-52; 19:38-42), their liberties, and even their lives (Rom. 16:3-4; Philp. 2:25-30), despite the displeasure and fury of their blood relatives and the governments under which they lived—all this for the spiritual advantage that accrued to them by their faithful adherence to his holy doctrine. True, many would have excused their following

NO CROSS, NO CROWN

of him, as mentioned in the parable of the feast (Luke 14:18-20). Some had bought land and would not come to the banquet. Some had married wives and wouldn't attend. And others had purchased yokes of oxen, and they would not come. All of these excuses sprang from an immoderate love of the world (2 Tim. 4:10). That was what hindered them. It was their "lawful" enjoyments. They served their "idols." They worshiped them more than God, and they would not give them up to come to God. This was recorded to their shame. In such things we see the power of "self" upon worldly man, and the danger that comes upon him by the abuse of lawful things.

Is your wife more dear to you than your Savior? Or, is your land or your cattle more precious to you than your soul's salvation? Be careful that your "creature comforts" do not prove to be traps for you, and then eventually a curse. Don't over-rate those things! Doing so is to provoke God who gave them to you (1 Cor. 4:7b). He can take them back just as easily (Dan. 4:19-37). So, come and follow Christ who gives eternal life to your soul.

THE DANGER OF CHOOSING YOUR "SELF"

WOE TO THOSE WHO have their hearts bound up in their earthly possessions (Luke 12:15). When those things are gone, then their so-called "heaven" is gone with them (Luke 16:9-12). Most of the people of the world stick with the comforts of this world. It is lamentable to see how their affections are mired and entangled with their "conveniences" of this life. The true, self-denying man is only a pilgrim. But the selfish man thinks that he is a "permanent" resident of this earth. Contrast the two types of people. One uses things as mere tools, as men do ships. They transport themselves or their equipment on a journey, that is, to get home. But the other one, the selfish one, looks no further than to be fixed in fullness and to attain comfort here. He likes it so much that, if he could, he would not trade anything for his lifestyle. However, he will not trouble himself to think of the other world (the afterlife), until he is sure that he can no longer live in this world. But alas, it'll be too late then. He won't be going to where Abraham is. Instead, he'll be joining "the rich man." This story is as sad as it is true.

This account is told in Luke 16:19-31: "Jesus said, 'There was a rich man who always dressed up in the finest clothes. He was so rich that he was able to feast and have a party every day. There was also a beggar named Lazarus. His body was covered with sores. He was often put at the rich man's gate. Lazarus only wanted to eat the crumbs which fell from the rich man's table. Instead, the dogs came and licked his sores! After a while, Lazarus died. The angels took Lazarus and placed him in the arms of Abraham. The rich man also died and was buried. He was sent to Hades and was in much pain. The rich man saw Abraham far away, with Lazarus in his arms. He called out, "Father Abraham, have mercy on me! Send Lazarus to me, so that he may dip the tip of his finger in water and cool my tongue. I am suffering in this fire!" But Abraham said, "My child, do you remember when you lived on earth? You had all the good things in life, but all the bad things happened to Lazarus. Now he is comforted here, and you are suffering. Also, there is a great canyon established between you and us. No one can cross over to help you; and no one can come over here from there." The rich man said, "Then father Abraham, please send Lazarus to my father's house on earth! I have five brothers. Lazarus could warn my brothers, so that they won't come to this place of pain." But Abraham said, "They have Moses and the prophets to read; let them learn from that!" But the rich man said, "No, father Abraham! If only some-one could come back to them from death, then they would change their hearts." But Abraham said to him, "No! If your brothers won't listen to Moses and the prophets, then they wouldn't be persuaded by anyone who might come back from death!" ' "

THE REWARDS OF SELF-DENIAL

HOWEVER, THAT STORY IS profitable for the disciples of Jesus who deny themselves. Indeed, Christ himself had that eternal joy in his eye: "Because of the happiness that lay ahead for him. He didn't mind the way he had to die" (Heb. 12:2). Jesus denied himself, and he bore the reproaches of the wicked. "He despised the shame," namely, the dishonor and derision of the world. It did not make him afraid, nor did he shrink back. He condemned it and he is now sitting at the right hand of the throne of God (Heb. 1:3). Peter once asked Christ: "Look, we have left everything and followed you! What will there be for us?" Jesus said to them, "I am telling you the truth: You have followed me. At the time when things will be made right, when I sit on my glorious throne, you will also sit on twelve thrones. You will judge the twelve tribes of Israel. Every person who has left his home, brothers, sisters, father, mother, children, or fields, because of my name, will receive many rewards and, after that person dies, he will receive eternal life with God." (Matt. 19:27-29). That was the lot of his disciples. It was this promised reward, this eternal "crown of righteousness" (2 Tim. 4:8), that in every age has been raised in the souls of the righteous to produce a holy neglect, yes, even a contempt of this world. This was what sustained the martyrs when they died for the triumph of the truth.

ABRAHAM'S EXAMPLE

THIS IS NOT A new doctrine. It is as old as Abraham. His life was made up of several remarkable instances of self-denial. First, he forsook his own native land of Chaldea. We can assume that he was settled there in a place of abundance. Why did he do it? Because God called him. Indeed, that should be reason enough, but, according to the world's depravity, it was not. Sometimes they pretend to admire their ancestors, but people today would make fun of Abraham for leaving a comfortable home. Folks despise what they don't understand.

But Abraham obeyed God. And so, God gave him a wonderful, fertile land. That was the first reward for his obedience. The next reward was a son born in Abraham's old age. It was a miracle because this took place after the normal time of his wife's ability to give birth to children. Nevertheless, God arranged for this special child (Isaac), their only child, the joy of their old age, the son of a miracle, and the one upon whom the fulfilling of the promise made to Abraham did depend. Concerning this son, I say, God tested Abraham. It might have overturned Abraham's faith and caused his integrity to falter. It might have caused Abraham to have serious doubts. God's clear command seemed unreasonable and cruel. (That was from the tempter's viewpoint—it could not be so from God's vantage point!) Perhaps Abraham was thinking, "Did God give me a son just to make a sacrifice of him!? Should a father be a butcher of his only child!? Is God requiring me to offer up the son of His own promise, by whom His covenant is to be performed. That's incredible!" Abraham might have rationalized that way. He could have resisted the voice of God and indulged his great affections for his beloved Isaac. But good old Abraham knew the Voice who had promised him a son. Abraham had not forgotten to recognize that same Voice when it commanded him again. He did not dispute it, even though the situation looked strange, surprising, and filled with horror (from a human point of view). Abraham had learned to believe that the same God who gave him a child by a miracle could also work another miracle to preserve that boy or restore him (Rom. 4:18-21). Abraham's affections could not outweigh his duty, much less overcome his faith. Abraham never doubted anything that God promised to him!

Abraham bowed to the voice of the Almighty and he built an altar, and he bound his only son upon that altar. Yes, it was Abraham who spread that fire and stretched forth his hand to take the knife. But the angel stopped the plunging of that knife. "Hold on, Abraham, your integrity has been

NO CROSS, NO CROWN

proven!" And what happened next? A ram served as the substitute (Gen. 22:1-13). Isaac was his again. When everything is consigned to God, this example shows how much more valuable the sacrifice is to the Almighty One. God is seeking one's whole heart. *That* is what pleases Him. So, it is not the sacrifice that recommends the heart, but the heart that gives the sacrifice acceptance. Long, long ago the prophet Hosea wrote these words for God:

> "I want faithful love
> > more than I desire animal sacrifices.
> I want people to know Me
> > more than I desire whole burnt-offerings."

God often seeks our best comforts and calls for what we love most but are least willing to part with. Not that He always takes it utterly away, but, He does this to test our soul's integrity, to caution us from excesses, and so that we may remember Him, the Author of those blessings that we "possess." We can learn to live without those things, if necessary.

I speak my experience: The way to keep the things that we enjoy on this earth is to resign them to God. Though that is hard, it is sweeter to see them returned, just as Isaac was restored to his father Abraham. Abraham loved Isaac more after that test, and Abraham appreciated the blessing of Isaac even more than he did before going to Mount Moriah.

O stupid world! O worldly Christians, not only strangers, but enemies to this excellent faith! As long as you act that way, you can never know the rewards that God has in store for you!

JOB'S EXAMPLE

JOB'S SELF-DENIAL WAS ALSO very significant. For when the messengers of his afflictions leaned hard upon him, one doleful story after another, until he was left almost as naked as when he was born, what did Job do? The first thing he did was to fall to the ground and to worship God (Job 1:20). Job kissed the hand of God that had stripped him! And, as far as complaining went, Job summarized his losses of real estate and his children with these words: "I was naked when I was born. And, I will be naked when I die. Yahweh gave these to me. And, He has taken them away. Praise be to the Name of Yahweh!" (Job 1:21). O the deep faith, patience, and contentment of this excellent man! One would have thought that this repeated news of ruin would have been enough to offset his confidence in God, but it did not. Instead, it steadied him. Indeed, Job tells us why. He believed in the resurrection. He knew that his Redeemer (Hebrew: *go'el*, his near-kinsman) lived. Job said, "I know that my Defender is alive. And, I know that, in the end, *he* will come to stand up for me. Even after my skin rots in the ground, I will still see God away from my flesh." (Job 19:25-26). It appears that Job's "Redeemer" did rescue him, because He had redeemed him from the world. Job's heart was not in his worldly comforts. Job's hope lived above the joys of time and the troubles of mortality. Job was not tempted by the one or shaken by the other. No, Job firmly believed that, after the worms would have consumed his body, his eyes would see his God. Thus, was the heart of Job. It submitted to and was comforted in the will of God!

MOSES' EXAMPLE

MOSES IS THE NEXT great example in the sacred story of remarkable self-denials, long before Christ's appearance in the flesh. When Moses was an infant, he had been saved by God's extraordinary providence (Acts 7:18-21). The compassion of Pharaoh's daughter was the means of his preservation. The king of Egypt had decreed that all the Hebrew male babies be slaughtered (Exo. 1:15-16). But she adopted the baby Moses as her son, and she gave him the education of her father's court (Acts 7:22). Moses' own graceful presence and extraordinary abilities, joined with her love for him, and interest in her Egyptian father to promote him, must have rendered him, if not capable of succession, at least of being Chief Minister of Affairs under that wealthy and powerful prince. For Egypt was then, what Athens and Rome later became, the most famous center for learning, art, and splendor.

But Moses was ordained for another work and guided by a higher principle. His years of discretion came. He realized the injustice of Egypt. He saw the oppression of his Hebrew brethren there. This became a burden that was too heavy for him to bear. This wise and good man could not want those generous and grateful acknowledgments that became the kindness of the king's daughter to him. Instead, he saw the God that was invisible. The writer of the Letter to the Hebrews put it this way: "By faith, when Moses had grown up, he said no to being called 'Pharaoh's daughter's son.' God's people were being mistreated. Moses chose to be mistreated also, instead of having fun for a while doing sinful things. Suffering shame for the Messiah was more important to Moses than the rich treasures of Egypt. He was looking ahead to the reward. By faith, Moses left Egypt behind. He was not afraid of making the king angry. Moses kept going toward the unseen One, as though he could see Him" (Heb. 11:24-27).

Moses did not dare to live in the ease and abundance of Pharaoh's house while his poor brethren were required to make bricks without straw (Exo. 5:7,16).

So, the reverence for Almighty God took a deep hold of his heart, and he nobly refused the status of Egyptian nobility. Instead, Moses chose a life of affliction, along with the most despised and oppressed Israelites. And he chose to be the companion of their tribulations and dangers than "to enjoy the pleasures of sin for a season; esteeming the reproaches of Christ," which he suffered for making that unworldly choice. Moses had greater riches than all the treasures of that earthly kingdom!

Moses was not foolish, as they thought him to be. He had reason on his side, for it is said, he had an eye for the ultimate reward. Moses refused the lesser benefit for the greater one. His wisdom transcended that of the Egyptians. They had made the present world their choice, though it was as uncertain as the weather. No, Moses looked deeper, and he weighed the pleasures of this life on the scales of eternity, and he found that they have no weight at all there. Moses governed himself not by the immediate possession but by the nature and duration of the reward. His faith corrected his affections, and it taught him to sacrifice the pleasures of "self" for the hope which he had of a future, more excellent reward.

OTHER EXAMPLES

ISAIAH IS ANOTHER INSTANCE of this blessed example of self-denial. He was a courtier who became a prophet of God. He left behind the worldly interests of one for the faith, patience, and sufferings of the other. His choice caused him to lose the favor of men, but their wickedness was enraged at his integrity, and in his fervent and bold reproofs of them. In the end, they made a martyr of him. They barbarously sawed him in two during the reign of King Manasseh (Heb. 11:37b). That's how that wonderful man died. Isaiah is commonly called "the evangelical prophet."

I will add one more example, though there could be many more. That example is the faithfulness of Daniel, a holy and wise young man. When his external advantages competed with his duty to Almighty God, Daniel relinquished them all. Instead of being desirous of how to secure himself, and to think of nothing else, to the utmost hazard to himself, Daniel was very careful to preserve the honor of God by his faithfulness to God's will. Though such a stance exposed Daniel to possible ruination at first, in the end, it advanced him tremendously in the world of the Middle East. This was an instance of great encouragement to all who want to be just like him. They will choose to keep a good conscience even during trying times. Even in the eyes of pagan kings, the God of Daniel was made famous and awesome through Daniel's perseverance.

What should I say of all the rest who did not regard anything more dear than doing the will of God? They abandoned their worldly comforts, and they exposed their ease and safety. They did it as often as the heavenly vision called upon them to do so, even when the wrath and malice of degenerate princes and an apostate church threatened them. The prophets Jeremiah, Ezekiel, and Micah denied themselves in obedience to the Divine Voice, thereby sealing their testimony with their own blood.

Self-denial was the practice and glory of the ancient saints. They were the predecessors to the coming of Christ in the flesh. How could we ever hope to go to heaven without self-denial now!? Our Savior himself has become the most excellent example of self-denial. Some today pretend to have this trait or claim that we don't need it. But for us, denying ourselves is the only way to be true followers of Jesus' blessed example (1 Pet. 2:21).

EVERYTHING MUST BE ABANDONED FOR CHRIST

THEREFORE, WHOEVER YOU ARE that would do the will of God but fail in your desires because of the opposition of worldly considerations, remember this: I am telling you, in the name of Christ, the one who gives preference to father or mother, sister or brother, wife or child, house or land, reputation, honor, office, liberty, or life—in opposition to the testimony of the light of Jesus in his own conscience—that individual will be rejected by Christ at the solemn and general judgment of the world, when everyone will be judged. That person will receive according to the deeds done in this life, not by what one professes to be! Jesus taught, that if your right hand offends you, you must cut it off. And if your right eye offends you, then you must pluck it out. Here is the wording of Matt. 5:29-30: "If your right eye is making you sin, take it out and throw it away from you! You would be better off to destroy one part of your body than to have your whole body thrown into hell. Or, if your right hand is making you sin, cut it off and throw it away from you! You would be better off to destroy one member of your body than for your whole body to go off into hell."

This means that, if the most precious, the most useful or tender comforts that you enjoyed, stand in your soul's way, and if it interrupts your obedience to the voice of God, and your conformity to His holy Word, then you need to get rid of any of these hindrances. If you don't part with such things, they could damn your soul!

The way of God is a way of faith. The Apostle Paul says that obedient children regard all things as "garbage," so that they may win Christ (Philp. 3:8), and know him (Philp. 3:10) and walk in his narrow way (Matt. 7:13-14). Speculation will not do, nor can refined notions enter in. Only the obedient are allowed to eat the good things of this land, says Isaiah: " 'If you people are willing to obey Me, then you will eat good crops from the land. But if you refuse to obey, and if you turn against Me, then you will be destroyed by the swords of your enemies.' Yahweh Himself said these things" (Isa. 1:19-20).

Those who do his will, says the blessed Jesus, will know of this doctrine: "If anyone wants to do what God wants, that person will find out whether my teaching comes from God or if I am speaking on my own" (John 7:17). Jesus will instruct them. But wherever lawful "self" is lord, there is no room for Christ's instruction. "Self" does not want to serve Christ, because "self" cannot receive his teaching. A person might think: "O what would my father or mother say? How would my husband treat me? Or, what would a government official do to me? Even though I have a very strong faith and clear conviction upon my soul about this or that thing, yet considering how unconventional it is, what enemies it has, and how strange and weird I would seem to people, I hope that God will pity my weakness if I falter. I am only human. Maybe later God could give me more strength. There is time enough." That's the way a selfish, fearful person rationalizes.

Deliberating only makes it worse, because the soul will lose the argument in vacillation. The proof is in the pudding! God never convinced anyone *until* they submitted. Then He empowered them. God requires nothing of us without giving us the ability to perform the task. Let's not mock God. Let's save people. Just do your duty (Luke 17:10). God shows you your duty, provided you partake of that light and spirit by which He gives you that insight. Some simply want power but they won't receive Christ in their souls (John 1:11-12). Like those in ancient times, to truly become the children of God (John 1:13), it is through the pure obedience of faith (Rom. 1:5).

A FINAL EXHORTATION

THEREFORE, LET ME IMPLORE you, by the love and mercy of God, by the life and death of Christ, by the power of His Spirit, and the hope of immortality, that you—if your hearts are firmly established in your temporal comforts, and you are lovers of "self" (2 Tim. 3:2,4) more than of these heavenly things—that you, that is, your hearts not be drawn away from the fear, love, obedience, and self-denial of becoming a true follower of Jesus. So, turn around and listen to the "still, small voice" (1 Kings 19:12) in your conscience. It tells you what your sins are and that you are miserable in them. It gives you a lively discovery of the vanity of the world, and it opens to the soul some prospect of eternity, and the comfort of the righteous ones who are already at rest in heaven. If you heed your conscience, it will divorce you from sin and "self." You will soon find that the power of its moral charms exceeds that of the wealth, honor, and beauty of this world. Finally, it will give you that tranquility which the storms of time can never wreck or ruin. Here all of your enjoyments are blessed, though small, yet great by that presence that is within them.

Even in this world the righteous have the advantage, because they use the world but don't abuse it. They see and bless the heavenly Hand that feeds them. They wear simple clothes, and they preserve them. And they behold the handiwork of God, but they don't adore them, only Him. So, the sweetness of God's blessings that gives them is an advantage over those who do not see God. Besides, the prosperous, righteous ones are not lifted up in pride nor are they cast down by their adversities. Why? Because, by God's divine presence, they are moderated in the one and comforted in the other.

In short, heaven is God's throne, and the earth is only the footstool of that person who has "self" under control. And those who know that principle will not be easily moved. Such people do learn "to number their days" (Psalms 90:12). They will not be surprised with their plight. Instead, they redeem their time, because the days are evil (Eph. 5:16). Or, to put it another way, "Take advantage of every opportunity, because these are evil times." They remember that they are only stewards, and that they must be accountable to an impartial, heavenly Judge. Therefore, they live for God, not for "self." And they die in the Lord, and they are blessed with those "who die in the Lord" (Rev. 14:13).

CHAPTER 4

Worshiping God

I NOW RETURN TO THE subject of the unlawful "self," which is the main concern of the great majority of mankind. It's a two-fold topic. First, this brand of "selfishness" even affects one's worship to God. Second, "self-centeredness" touches on the ethics of everyday living. We need to realize that both aspects have far-reaching consequences. I will try to be as brief as possible in discussing this but still cover the subject adequately.

"Selfishness" in religion ought to have been put to death by the cross of Christ. But man's clever inventiveness injects itself into a starring role. Man loves to *perform* his worship toward God. So, contrived worship is not holy at all! These deceived people call themselves by the name of "Christian," but their worship consists only of external, pompous, and superstitious acts of worship! These people are not spiritually prepared to truly worship God Almighty who is an eternal Spirit (John 4:24). Their version of worship is composed of what is utterly inconsistent with the very form and practice of Christ's doctrine. The examples of apostolic worship were simple and spiritual, but modern churches are gaudy and worldly. Christ's worship was inward and mental, but the "worship" of today is mostly outward and physical. True worship is suited to the nature of God (John 4:23) who is spirit. Their false worship is quite carnal. Instead of emphasizing the spiritual aspects of true worship, behold, they cater to gratify flesh and blood, as if the purpose was to please *them*, not God!

These current pretenders have produced a "worship" that is bedecked with stately cathedrals, church buildings, elaborate imagery, rich furniture, vestments, special voices, instrumental music, expensive lamps, wax candles, and incense. Everything is fully orchestrated and designed to appeal to whatever artistic tastes that human senses crave or that money can buy. Are they trying to recreate an ancient Jewish gallery or an Egyptian museum? Do they think that God is an old man? Is Christ a little boy who needs to be entertained at a party with masks!? That's how they portray Jesus in their "sanctuaries," and that's the way that too many people think of him. The truth is, because people are making God "in their *own* image" (compare Gen. 1:26), their worship imitates what they imagine God to be. That is their idea of God, and that's why they address God the way they do. They like this kind of ostentatious "worship," so they think that God likes it, too!

ACCEPTABLE WORSHIP

BUT WHAT DID THE Almighty One say to ancient people who were guided by similar sensibilities? Psalms 50:21-23 says:

> "I have kept quiet while you did these things.
> You thought I was just like you.
> But I will reprimand you.
> I will accuse you to your face!

Think about this, you people who forget God.
Otherwise, I will tear you apart,
and no one will save you.
The person who honors Me
is the one who gives Me offerings to show thanks.
And I, God, will save one who does that!"

What is acceptable worship to God? The prophet Micah answers: "O man, Yahweh has told you what is good, and what He seeks of you: Treat other people fairly. Love mercy. And live humbly with your God" (Micah 6:8). For the One who searches the heart and tests the emotions of men (Jer. 17:10) is the One who displays man's sins right in front of him. He is "the God of the spirits of all flesh" (Num. 16:22; 27:16). He is the One who does not look at the external fabric but the internal frame of the soul and the inclination of the heart (1 Sam. 16:7). The Psalmist describes God this way:

"O Yahweh, my God, You are very great.
You are clothed with splendor and majesty.
You wear light like a robe.
You stretch out the skies like a tent.
You build Your own room above the clouds.
You make the clouds Your chariot.
You ride on the wings of the wind.
You make the winds Your messengers.
Flames of fire are Your servants.
You set the earth on its foundations,
so that it can never be moved" (Psalms 104:1-5).

God cannot be adequately worshiped by purely contrived human inventions. No, such things are only the refuge of an apostate people who departed (1 Tim. 4:1-3) from the primitive power of religion and the spirituality of authentic Christian worship.

SPIRITUAL WORSHIP

CHRIST PULLED HIS DISCIPLES away from the "splendor" and "worship" of the external temple of Herod (Matt. 24:1-2). Instead, Christ initiated a more inward and spiritual type of worship. He instructed his followers about a superior concept. For example, Christ said to the Samaritan woman: "Believe me, woman, the time is coming when you won't worship the Father on this mountain or in Jerusalem. . . . God is spirit. The people who worship God must worship Him in the true way and with the right spirit" (John 4:21,24). What was Jesus really saying? It was because of the weakness of early people that God condescended to be worshiped in primitive ways in ancient times, limiting Himself to an outward time, place, temple, and priesthood. But that was during a time when men were ignorant (Acts 17:30) of God's omnipresence. They didn't understand what God is or where He is. Jesus came to reveal God to as many people as could receive this message. People must first be acquainted with God as "spirit" in order to comprehend Him and worship Him as such. It is not tactile worship or ritualistic ceremonies ("the worship services") which are in use among us today. Employing such liturgy is not really serving God. No, you must obey His Spirit who strives within you (Gen. 6:3), gathering you out of the evils of this world to bow to his instructions and commands in your own souls. That is how you may know what it is to worship God as "spirit" (John 4:23-24). Then you will understand that it is *not* going to this mountain or to Mount Zion in Jerusalem. Instead, it is doing the will of God, keeping His commandments, and communing within your own heart, and not sinning. It is taking up your cross (Matt. 16:24), meditating on His holy law (Psalms 1:2; 119:97), and following the example of Christ (John 13:15) whom the Father has sent (John 5:23,30).

Consider the example of Stephen, that bold and faithful martyr of Jesus in Acts 6 and Acts 7. He was falsely accused of blasphemy. When Stephen was a prisoner on trial for disputing the purpose of their beloved "temple" and its "services", Stephen told those Jews, "Solomon built God a House. However, the Highest One does not live in houses which men build with their hands" (Acts 7:47-48). This is what the prophet Isaiah wrote:

> "This is what Yahweh says:
> 'Heaven is My throne,
> and the earth is My footstool.
> So, do you think you can build a House for Me? No.
> There is no place where I need to rest.
> My hand made all these things.
> All these things exist because of Me.
> These are the kind of people whom I am pleased with:
> those who are not proud or stubborn;
> those who revere Me.' " (Isa. 66:1-2)

Behold, the foregoing passage of Scripture constitutes a total overthrow of all worldly temples and their ceremonial trappings!

That beloved martyr continued his assault upon those apostate Jews (those pompous, ceremonious, worldly worshipers) with these words: "You stubborn leaders! Your hearts are not circumcised! You won't listen to God! You are always against what the Holy Spirit is trying to tell you. Your ancestors did this, and you are just like them!" (Acts 7:51).

It is as if God Himself were telling them: "Your outward temples, rites, and shadowy services (Heb. 8:5) don't matter. Neither do your pretensions to be successors of Abraham (Matt. 3:9; 8:53) or the protectors of the religion of Moses (John 9:28). You people are resisting the Holy Spirit, and contradicting his explicit instructions. You won't bow to his counsel, and your hearts are not right toward God. You are the successors of your forefathers' iniquity. Though you verbally admire your ancestors, yet none of you, in your faith and life, are the successors of the true prophets!

The prophet Isaiah carried it a little farther than what Stephen said. For after having declared what is not God's House (the place where God's Name dwells), Isaiah wrote these stinging words: "But to this man will I look, even to him that is poor, and of a contrite spirit, and trembles at my Word" (Isa. 66:2).

O carnal and superstitious man, you need to become a true worshiper and to understand the true place of God's rest! It's the sanctuary of the One whom "heaven and the heaven of heavens cannot contain" (1 Kings 8:27). Man's "self" cannot build it, nor can the art or power of man prepare or consecrate it!

TRUE WORSHIP

IN TWO INSTANCES, PAUL, that great Apostle of the Gentiles, specifically used the word "temple" (Greek: *naos*), when he referred to human beings. In Paul's First Epistle to the congregation at Corinth he said, "Surely you realize that your body is a temple sanctuary? You have received the Holy Spirit from God. The Holy Spirit is inside you—in the temple sanctuary. You don't belong to yourselves" (1 Cor. 6:19). You see, "temple" here in this passage was *not* a building! Again, in Paul's Second Letter to them, he told the same people: "*We* are the sanctuary of the living God!" (2 Cor. 6:16). Then Paul cited God's words through the prophet Moses, "I will always walk among you and be your God. And, you will be My people." (Lev. 26:12) *This* is the evangelical temple, the Christian church (*ekklesia*), whose ornaments are not the embroideries and furniture of worldly art and wealth, but "the fruits of the Spirit" (Gal. 5:22-23; Eph. 5:9), such as meekness, love, faith, patience, and self-denial. Herein is the eternal Wisdom that was with God from a time before eternity began:

"I, Wisdom, was with the Always-Present One
when He began His creative work,
before He made anything else in ancient times.
I was appointed in the very beginning,
even before the world began.
I began before the mountains had been shaped.
I was born before the hills had ever been put in place.
I enjoyed His whole world.
And, I was happy with all its people" (Prov. 8:22,23,25,31).

God does not live in houses built of wood and stone. His living House (Rom. 12:1-2) is more glorious than Solomon's dead house. Christ is the one who built up a holy temple to God (see Eph. 2:19-21). In ancient times, the glory of the latter House (Christ's people) was supposed to transcend the glory of the former house (Solomon's temple), says the prophet Haggai:

"This is what Yahweh of the armies of heaven says: 'In a short time, I will shake the heavens and the earth once again. And, I will shake the ocean and the dry land. And, I will shake all the nations. The One yearned for[1] by all the nations will come. Then I will fill this temple with splendor.' says Yahweh of the armies of heaven. 'The silver is Mine, and the gold is Mine.' says Yahweh of the armies of heaven. 'The latter splendor of this temple shall be greater than the former splendor.' says Yahweh of the armies of heaven. 'And, in this place, I will give peace,' says Yahweh of the armies of heaven" (Hag. 2:6-9).

The words above apply to those who would try to outdo one another in building elaborate church buildings. What good does that do!? But the divine glory, the beauty of holiness in the gospel House (the *ekklesia* of Christ), which is made up of renewed believers, far exceeds the outward glory of Solomon's temple!

1   the Messiah

SIMPLE PLACES TO MEET

BUT FOR ALL THIS, true Christians do have some adequate meeting-places. They are plain, simple, and devoid of pomp or ceremony. God's presence is not with the edifice, but with those who are in it. They are the *ekklesia*, not the building. O that those who call themselves "Christians" knew that real sanctity is *within* them by "the washing of God's regenerating mercy" (Titus 3:5) instead of that imaginary "holiness" ascribed to physical places! Then they would know what "the church" really is, and where the place of God's appearance is in this Christian age. This caused David to say, "The princess is very beautiful. Her gown is woven with golden thread" (Psalms 45:13).[2] What is the glory that is within the true *ekklesia* (= the body of Christ, Eph. 1:22-23; Col. 1:18,24), and that gold which makes up that inward glory? O superstitious man, tell me. Is it your stately temples, altars, tables, carpets, or tapestries? Could it be the sacred vestments, organs, choirs, pulpits, pews, candles, lamps, censers, jewels, or collection plates of your worldly temples? No! They bear no resemblance to the blessed, redeemed *ekklesia* of Christ. What a miserable apostasy your churches are! What happened to the apostolic pattern of the Book of Acts? Where is the spiritual glory of that first century *ekklesia*?

CROSSES AND CRUCIFIXES

WHY HAVE THEY ERECTED so many crosses? How can we hope to justify the proliferation of crucifixes or reconcile these "trinkets" with true Christianity!? The closer the sculpted images are to being life-like, the further away they are from spiritual reality. It's true, they've got crosses, but they are trying to replace the real cross of Christ. Those who wear crosses

2   This refers to the children of God throughout all the ages. Compare Revelation 19:7-8; 21:2,9.

ought to be *carrying* them! Instead of crucifying their wills, their crosses have become mere jewelry without meaning. So, the cross is their "sign" that does nothing but tell the world that they are "Christian" in some vague sense.

Some people think that, if they wear so-called "holy" objects (such as a crucifix around one's neck or other "sacred" jewelry) or they practice formal liturgies and display the appropriate outward signs in worship, then they are "lovers" of the cross of Jesus. Do we need more church spires? Do these things make people more like Christ? Such may appear to the world that way, but in reality they have strayed far from the main message of Christ's cross, that is, self-denial! Man does what *he* wants, not what is pleasing to God. The true disciple of Christ is not trying to do his own will but the will of the heavenly Father!

The cross-symbol is the kind of cross that flesh and blood can carry because human beings invented it, but it is *not* the real cross of Christ, which deals with crucifying our will (Gal. 2:19-20). Thousands of these wooden crosses have no more virtue than a single wood chip! They are but poor, empty shadows that do not reflect the image of the true cross. Some people carry their little crosses as good-luck charms. They are like expensive gems, the spoils of superstition, in the people's pockets or purses. But those objects never repel even one sin! Their owners still commit sin while they have them on their person. Though they may clutch them to their bosoms, their beloved lusts lie there too. All this, without the least twinge in their consciences. These crucifixes are as mute as the fake gods that Elijah exposed (1 Kings 18:27). There's no life or power in them. And how could those material things, whose likeness and workmanship are traceable to the labor of worldly artists, be effective? Do these crosses mend their makers? Surely not!

These crosses and crucifixes are yokes without restraint that never contradict us. A whole cart-load of them would never lead one person to repentance. People may as well knock their brains out with them; they won't solve sins! I fear that too many people who use them know the difference in their consciences. Indeed, they regard them with "adoration." This can only happen to false crosses. These worshipers are so proud of them. But the true cross allows for no false pride (1 Cor. 1:29; 3:21; 4:7; 9:16), whenever it is truly carried (Matt. 16:24).

As their religion is, so are their crosses—garish and pretentious. But what do they signify? These venerated idols are often made of earthly treasures such as precious metals. Instead of teaching the people who wear those crosses to deny themselves, these manufactured crosses are respected for their finery! An expensive cross will attract many admirers, but ordinary ones are overlooked. I could argue with these adherents that such a cross is superstitious, not like the blessed cross of Jesus which takes away our sins (Col. 2:13-14). The cross of Christ was never meant to be a "medal of honor" to show off!

THE CLOISTERED LIFE

A RECLUSIVE LIFE (THAT is, the boasted "righteousness" of some) is not more commendable than righteous living in the world. Such devotees are more ignorant than virtuous. They're trying to escape from the world by abandoning it! They want to stay completely out of the range of temptation. If they don't see sin, they believe that their hearts won't crave sin. But if you are not tempted, you won't ever be tested (Rom. 16:10; 1 Cor. 3:13-14; 2 Cor. 8:2; 13:5; Philp. 2:22; 1 Thess. 2:4; 2 Tim. 2:15; Heb. 11:17; James 1:3,12; 1 Pet. 1:7; Rev. 2:10) Withdrawal is not one bit nearer to the nature of the true cross! Their kind of "self-denial" is lazy and unprofitable. Others are expected to take care of them. It's unnatural. True religion never taught this. The true "convent" or "monastery" is *within* a person where the spiritual soil is cloistered from sin. True followers of Christ can carry this religious "house" around with them. They don't have to exempt themselves from the real world, though they will try to keep themselves from the evils of the world (James 1:27d) by the way that they live.

Those who choose a cloistered environment (i.e., the convent, mon-astery, religious institution, etc.) think that they are pleasing or serving God better. But they are actually hiding from the world and the chance to take up their cross daily in society. They can never be tempted as long as they never expose themselves to the world where sin abounds. Therefore, they can never truly pick up the true cross of Christ. They are expected to be idle and deny certain things to themselves even though they do not consciously choose this. They are told what to do and when to do it by somebody else.

The cross of Christ is of an entirely different nature. A true Christian truly overcomes the world (1 John 5:4-5) and leads a life of purity in the face of its allurements. Those who carry it are not chained up for fear that they might bite somebody! Nor are they locked up lest they might be stolen away. No, they receive power directly from Christ, "the Captain of their salvation" (Heb. 2:10), to resist the Devil (James 4:7), and to do what is good (Gal. 6:10) in the sight of God; to despise the world (1 John 2:15-16), and to love its reproach (Matt. 5:11-12; 1 Pet. 2:12) above its praise (John 12:43); and not only not to offend others, but to love those who op-pose them and not hate them (Matt. 5:44).

What a world we would have if everybody, for fear of transgress-ing, were to confine himself within four walls! No, the perfection of the Christian life extends to every honest occupation in the world. This im-posed severity of their artificial "vows" does *not* emanate from Christ's free spirit but a willful, fleshly "humility" of their own making. It really makes no sense. Plainly, they are their own lawgivers. They set their own rules, penalties, and loop-holes. It is a constrained harshness which is out of touch with the rest of creation. But, sin spoils their world view.

True godliness does not literally direct people out of the world (1 Cor. 5:9-10). Instead, real piety enables them to live better lives within this world. It encourages their best efforts to mend it, not to hide their lamp under a bushel basket but to set it upon a lamp table (Matt. 5:15). Besides, withdrawing from the world is a selfish concoction. It could never be the true way of picking up the cross (Matt. 10:38; 16:24). The real cross is taken out to the people (Matt. 28:18-20)! But their reclusive attitude runs away to be isolated, abandoning the world behind to be lost. But true Christians should stay at the helm and guide the ship to its proper port. They should not sneak away at the stern, leaving the passengers without a pilot, to be driven by the fury of evil times upon the rocks of destruction or the sands of ruin.

Finally, this hermit sort of life, if adopted by young people, often disguises their laziness or their secret desire to gain a sense of "security." They may be in that refuge for a lifetime and yet still have guilty feelings. Paul wrote this: "None of these things will last after they have been used for a while. They are human commands and teachings. These things look like there is wisdom behind them. They have forced worship, false humility, and harsh treatment of the human body, but, they don't help control physical desires at all!" (Col. 2:22-23)

EXTERNAL RELIGION OR INNER DISCIPLINE?

BUT TAKING UP THE genuine cross of Jesus is an inner exercise. It is the discipline of the soul in conformity to the Divine Mind (Gal. 4:19). Doesn't the body follow the soul, and not the other way around? No cell can shut up the soul from lust. The sheltered life cannot prevent the mind from thinking of many unrighteous ideas. The thoughts of man's heart are continually evil (Gen. 6:5). Since evil comes from within, and not from the outside (Matt. 15:19), how then can an external application remove an internal cause? Or, how can an outer restraint upon the body work a confinement of the mind? The more time behind bars that a prisoner has to think about crime, the more trouble he will get into later. If his thoughts are not guided by a higher principle, he will not be rehabilitated. So, convents and monasteries are more damaging to the world than touching it.

I am not talking about a haven for rest. Occasional retreats are both beneficial and necessary. Sometimes you need to get away from crowds—but only temporarily.

Man, examine your faulty foundation! What is it and who placed you there on it? Otherwise, in the end, it would appear that you have cheated your own soul eternally! (I must confess that I am prejudiced for my Savior's kind of "righteousness" (Philp. 3:9), having found mercy with my heavenly Father.) I would not want anyone to deceive himself into destruction especially about religion which people are more apt to take for granted. The inward, steady "righteousness of God" (Rom. 3:22) is something different than all the contrived devotion of poor, superstitious people. Standing approved in the sight of God excels that physical exercise in religion resulting from the creations of men. And, the soul that is awakened and preserved by Christ's holy power and spirit lives for God in his own way and worships Him within his own spirit.

I'm not against "getting away from it all." I admire solitude. Christ himself was an example of it. He loved and chose to frequent mountains, gardens, and lakesides (Mark 6:31). It is necessary for spiritual growth. Divine pleasures can be found in free solitude. And I respect the virtue that seeks and uses solace properly. (I wish there was more of it in the world.) But it should be voluntary, not constrained. Meditation is not supposed to be a punishment in solitary confinement. Why don't they have more retreats for the afflicted, the tempted, the lonely individuals, and the devout so that they can wait upon God (Psalms 62:1,5) without being disturbed, and thereby be strengthened? They would become refreshed to enable them to go back into the world and face it head on!

CHAPTER 5

A New Attitude

*T*HERE ARE SOME REFORMERS who would not dare use (much less adore) a piece of wood or stone, or any image made of silver or gold. They wouldn't permit any Jewish style of worship, either. They wouldn't allow any pagan pomp in worship practiced by others. (Christ's worship is in this world, though his kingdom is from heaven.) These dogmatic reformers are doctrinally averse to such superstition, and yet they do not refrain from bowing down to their own religious duties, and esteeming their formal performance of several parts of the worship that goes against the grain of their fleshly ease. Also, they believe that, if they abstain from gross and scandalous sins, even though the thoughts about those sins are embraced, they regard themselves as safe enough to be within the circle of disciple-ship and the walls of Christianity. But this view is also below the discipline of Christ's cross. Those who flatter themselves with this sort of "carrying the cross" will eventually be deceived by walking on a sandy foundation (Matt. 7:26-27). Remember, Christ said: "I tell you, sometimes people talk without thinking. On the Judgment Day they will be held responsible for every word. Your words can make you right with God or your words can condemn you" (Matt. 12:36).

A HEART PREPARED BY THE SPIRIT OF GOD

FIRST, GOD LOOKS NOT at the performing of the duties of religion, but the motive behind the deeds. People often contradict themselves in their own wills—voluntary omission and commission. Long ago, Isaiah spoke these words on behalf of God to the Jews of his day: "You come to appear in front of Me. But who asked you to do all this running in and out of My courtyards?" (Isa. 1:12). Those seemingly "pious" Jews were ready enough to serve God, but their religiosity was only contrived, and in their own good time and will. It was not with a soul that was truly touched and prepared by the divine power of God. No, it was only outward, physical worship. The Apostle Paul tells us that that sort of thing profits little (1 Tim. 4:8). It is not in keeping with "taking up the cross" in worship, as well as in other things. Mere conformity is at the root of many troublesome superstitions which are still so widespread. People have not faced their sins or the implications of their brand of "worship." They see no need to change the way they live.

However, true worship can only come from a heart that has been prepared by the Lord (Prov. 16:1). This readiness comes from the sanctification of the Spirit. It is as Paul teaches in Rom. 8:14, "All people who are being led by God's Spirit are sons of God." Whatever prayer is made or whatever doctrine is uttered without the instigation of the Holy Spirit is not acceptable with God. It cannot be true, evangelical worship unless it is "in spirit and in truth" (John 4:23-24); that is, by the preparation and help of the Holy Spirit. Anything else, to God Almighty, is just a heap of pathetic words! God is Spirit, to whom words, places, and times, strictly considered, are improper and inadequate. And though they are the common instruments of public worship, they are only physical and visible. They cannot really carry our requests any higher to the invisible God. Are the words of your prayers directed to men or toward God (Matt. 6:5-15)? God hears the language of the soul: "We don't know how we should pray, but the Spirit helps our weakness. He personally talks to God for us with feelings which our language cannot express. God searches all people's hearts. He knows what the Spirit is thinking. The Spirit talks to God on behalf of holy people, using the manner which pleases God" (Rom. 8:26-27).

However lively the soul of man is in other things, it is dead to God until God breathes the spirit of life into it (Gen. 2:7). Man cannot live for Him, much less worship Him, without the soul (spirit). God tells us about this through Ezekiel's vision concerning the restoration of mankind (represented in Israel):

"Therefore, prophesy, and say to them: 'This is what the Lord Yahweh says: "Behold, O My people, I will open your graves. And, I will cause you to come up out of your graves. Then I will bring you back home, into the land of Israel. This is how you, O My people, will know that I am Yahweh! I will open your graves and cause you to come up from them. And, I will put My Spirit inside you. You will come to life. Then I will settle you in your own land. And, you will know that I, Yahweh, have spoken and done it!" ' says Yahweh" (Ezek. 37:12-14).

So, though Christ taught his disciples to pray (Luke 11:1-4), they were, in some ways, disciples *before* he taught them this. They were not worldly men whose prayers were an abomination to God (Prov. 28:9). And Jesus' teaching them a model prayer is not an argument that everybody must mindlessly recite a set prayer like "The Lord's Prayer," as is now too superstitiously practiced by rote. No, we are to pray now as He enables us to pray, just as He enabled them to pray.

We are not to "over-plan" what we're going to say when we come before worldly princes, because it will be given to us at that precise moment what to say or how to say it: "When they turn against you, don't worry about what or how you will speak. At that time what you should say will be given to you. *You* will not be doing the talking; it will be the Spirit of your heavenly Father who will be speaking through you" (Matt. 10:19-20).

We don't need to practice "saying" our prayers; God will help us to pray. He is our Father. So, the mouth of the body and the soul is shut until God opens it! And then He loves to hear the language that comes out of us. God's ear is always open to sincere petitions, and His Spirit strongly intercedes for those who offer them.

THE WAY TO PREPARE

HOW WILL THIS PREPARATION be obtained? I answer: By *waiting* patiently upon God, yet watchfully and intently.

The Psalmist says: "O Yahweh, You have heard what the poor people want. Do whatever they are asking for. Listen to them!" (Psalms 10:17).

And, Wisdom says: "People make plans in their hearts. But only the Always-Present One has the final word" (Prov. 16:1).

You must not think your own thoughts or speak your own words. No, prayer should be the silence of the holy cross. Seek sacred seclusion from all the confused imaginations that are likely to press upon your mind. It is not for you to think. Are you trying to overwhelm Almighty God with the eloquent words of your prayers? Are you looking for the most appropriate phrases? You shouldn't be. Just one groan, one sigh from a wounded soul, from a heart touched with true remorse is enough, provided that it is sincere, godly sorrow. That is the work of God's Spirit (2 Cor. 7:10). Therefore, "stand still" in your mind (Exo. 14:13). Simply wait to feel something that is divine, to prepare and compose yourself to worship God properly and acceptably. That is truly "taking up the cross" (Matt. 16:24). That is shutting the doors and windows of your soul to anything that might interrupt your attention in the presence of God. Regardless of your situation, the power of Almighty God can break in! His Spirit will work and prepare your heart so that it may offer up an acceptable sacrifice (Rom. 12:1-2).

God is the One who discovers and presses upon the desires of the soul. Whenever the soul of man cries out, He alone is the One who can supply the answers we seek. Petitions which do not spring from such a sense of preparation are too formal. They are not real because people pray ignorantly, using their own blind desires, and not pursuing the will of God. God's ear can't hear them because they are not praying according to His will. God has said:

"I will now rise up because the poor people are suffering" (Psalms 12:5).

These are the people who are "poor in spirit" (Matt. 5:3). These are the needy souls who really want His assistance. They are ready to be overwhelmed. They feel a need, and they cry aloud for a Deliverer, but they have no one on earth to help them. There is no one in the heavens or on the earth but God who can assist! David said:

"He will deliver the poor people when they cry out for help.
He will assist the needy people when no one else will help them.
He will redeem them from cruel people who would hurt them.
Their blood is so precious to Him" (Psalms 72:12,14).

King David also wrote:

"This poor man called out, and Yahweh heard him.
Yahweh saved him from all his troubles.
The angel of Yahweh camps around those who revere Him.
He delivers them" (Psalms 34:6-7).

The Sweet Psalmist of Israel invited everyone to come and taste how good the Lord is:

"He will bless those who revere Him,
from the smallest ones to the greatest ones" (Psalms 115:13).

BEING BROKEN IN SPIRIT

BUT WHAT IS THAT to those who are not hungry!? Jesus said, "Healthy people don't need a doctor, but sick people do" (Matt. 9:12). The full ones have no need to sigh. And the rich don't need to cry. Those who are not sensitive to their own inner needs, those who don't have any fears haunting them, those who feel no necessity for God's power to help them nor require the light of His countenance to comfort them, they won't pray. Their devotion is, at best, only a serious mockery of Almighty God. They know not, they want not, they desire not what they do pray for. They sometimes pray that the will of God "may be done" (Matt. 6:10), but they continue to do their own will! They ask for grace but abuse what they have. They pray for the Spirit, but they resist him within them, and they ridicule the Spirit in others. They request mercy and goodness from God but they feel no real need of either. And, in this inward insensibility, they are as unable to praise God for what they do have as to pray for what they have not.

David says:

"Those who look to Yahweh will praise Him" (Psalms 22:26).

"He satisfies the thirsty ones.
    He fills up the hungry people with good things"
    (Psalms 107:9).

God reserves good things for the poor and needy folks, and for those who revere God. Let the spiritually poor and the needy ones praise Your Name!

> "You who revere Yahweh, praise Him. And you, the seed of Jacob, glorify Him" (Psalms 22:23).

Jacob was a plain man, but he had an upright heart. His spiritual descendants are supposed to be like him. And though they may be as poor as worms in their own eyes, yet they should receive the strength to wrestle with God, and to prevail as he did (Gen. 32:23-32).

COMING INTO THE PRESENCE OF GOD

BUT WITHOUT THE ARRANGEMENT of and the consecration of the power of prayer, no one is fit to come before God. As far as holiness is concerned, there is no difference between the Old Testament and the New Testament: "You must be holy because I am holy!" (Lev. 11:44; 1 Pet. 1:16). All the sacrifices were "sprinkled" (i.e., made holy) *before* they were offered. The people dedicated whatever they offered *before* they presented themselves to the Lord (Num. 8:19; 2 Chron. 21:36; 30:16-17). If they touched a human corpse or any "unclean" animal, that very act caused the people to be unfit (ceremonially impure) for the temple or for sacrificing. How can we think of the worship that was instituted by Christ in the gospel age in such disrespectful terms!? Or, how can those who daily touch what is morally unclean (whether in thoughts, words, or deeds) worship the pure God acceptably without first coming to the blood of Jesus!? It sprinkles (purges) the conscience from dead works (Heb. 9:14). It's a downright contradiction! The unclean cannot acceptably worship what is holy (Lev. 10:10; Deut. 23:14); the impure cannot be near what is perfect! There *is* a holy connection and communion between Christ and his followers (1 Cor. 10:16-17). But there is no association at all between Christ and Belial or between Christ and those who disobey his commandments and do not live the life of his blessed cross of self-denial (2 Cor. 6:15-16).

Sin cannot worship God (Rom. 8:7-8). The prophet Micah cries out, acting the part of one who is in trouble:

> "You say:
>> 'What can I bring with me
>>> when I come into the presence of Yahweh?
>> What can I bring
>>> when I bow myself down before God on high?
>> Should I come into His presence with burnt-offerings
>>> or with year-old calves?
>> Would the Always-Present One be pleased with thousands
>>> of male sheep?
>>> Would He be pleased with 10,000 rivers of olive
>>>> oil?
>> Should I offer my firstborn child for my transgressions
>>> —the fruit of my womb for the sins of my life?'
>> O man, Yahweh has told you what is good,
>>> and what He seeks of you:
>> Treat other people fairly.
>> Love mercy.
>> And live humbly with your God" (Micah 6:6-8).

The royal prophet, David, who was sensitive to this, also implored God. David didn't dare open his lips after his sin of adultery with Bathsheba and after he murdered her husband. David knew that he could not bring himself to praise God at that particular time:

> "O Lord, let me speak,
>> so that I may praise You.
> You take no delight in sacrifices.

If You did, then I would offer them.
You do not savor a whole burnt-offering.
No, the sacrifice that God wants is a broken spirit.
O God, You will not reject
a heart that is broken and sorry for its sin"
(Psalms 51:15-17).

For the same reason, God Himself speaks through the mouth of Isaiah in opposition to the formalities and mere lip-service of the degenerate Jews:

"This is what Yahweh says:
'Heaven is My throne,
and the earth is My footstool.
So, do you think you can build a House for Me? No.
There is no place where I need to rest.
My hand made all these things.
All these things exist because of Me.'
says Yahweh.
"These are the kind of people whom I am pleased with:
those who are not proud or stubborn;
those who revere Me.' " (Isa. 66:1-2)

THE TRUE WORSHIPER

BEHOLD THE *TRUE* WORSHIPER! One of God's preparing, circumcised in heart (Deut. 10:16; 30:6; Jer. 4:4; Rom. 2:29) and ear, who does not resist the Holy Spirit (Acts 7:51), as those lofty, hypocritical Jews did. This was so then, even in the time of the law of Moses, which was the dispensation of external and shadowy performances (Heb. 10:1). Could we expect God to accept us today without the preparation of the Spirit of the Lord in these gospel times, which are the proper times for the outpouring of the Spirit (Acts 2:17-18; 10:45)? By no means! God is what He was, and His true worshipers are only those who worship Him "in spirit and in truth" (John 4:23-24). He takes care of these people as "the apple (the pupil) of His eye" (Psalms 17:8). The rest mock Him, and He despises them because of it (Prov. 1:22-27). Hear what will happen to those people, for it is the status quo and portion of so-called "Christendom" today:

> "But, those people who kill a bull as a sacrifice to Me insincerely
>   are like those who kill a human being.
> Those who kill a lamb as a sacrifice to Me insincerely
>   are like those who break the necks of dogs!
> Those who give Me so-called 'food-offerings'
>   are like those who offer Me the blood of pigs!
> Those who go through the motions of burning incense
>   are like those who worship idols!
> Those people choose their own ways—not Mine!
> In addition, they love the disgusting things that they do" (Isa. 66:3).

Let no one say: "We don't offer those kinds of oblations." That is not the case! God was not offended by the offerings but at the offerers! These were the legal forms of sacrifice appointed by God, but they were *not* presenting the sacrifices in the proper frame of spirit and with the right disposition of soul that was required. So, God declared His abhorrence of it. He was aggravated with them. Elsewhere, the same prophet told them not to bring any more vain oblations into God's presence:

> "Don't continue bringing Me worthless offerings!
>   I hate the incense that you burn.
> I cannot endure your New Moons, various sabbaths, and other
>   convocations.
> I cannot endure the evil that you do

in holding your so-called 'holy' meetings.
I hate your New Moon festivals
    and your other yearly festivals!
They have become like heavy weights on Me.
    I am tired of carrying them.
You will raise your arms in prayer to Me,
    but I will refuse to look at you.
Even if you say many prayers,
    I will not listen to you.
It is because your hands are full of blood!" (Isa. 1:13-15)

This was a stinging renunciation of their Jewish worship. Why? Because their hearts were polluted! They did not love the Lord with their whole hearts at all (Deut. 6:4-5). Instead, they broke His law, and they rebelled against His Spirit. They didn't do what was right in His sight. The cause was plain. Isaiah continued:

"Wash yourselves and make yourselves clean.
    Stop doing the evil things which I see you doing.
Stop doing wrong!
    Learn to do good!
Be fair to other people.
    Punish those who hurt others.
Help the orphans.
    Stand up for the rights of widows" (Isa. 1:16-17).

Upon these terms, and nothing short of them, Yahweh bids them to come to Him, and He tells them:

"Come, let's talk these things over.
Your sins are red,
    but they can be as white as snow.

Your sins are bright red,
>> but they can be white like wool" (Isa. 1:18).

So true is that notable passage from the Psalmist:

"All of you who revere God, come and listen.
>> I will tell you what He has done for me.
I cried out loud to Him with my mouth.
>> I glorified Him with my tongue.
If I had cherished any sin in my heart,
>> then the Lord would not have listened to me.
But God has truly listened.
>> He has paid attention to the sound of my prayer.
Praise God!
>> He did not ignore my prayer.
He did not hold back His constant love from me"
(Psalms 66:16-20).

DAVID'S EXAMPLE

MORE PASSAGES OF THIS kind could be cited to show the displeasure of God against His own prescribed forms of worship but which were being performed without His Spirit, as well as the necessary preparation of the heart in man. David, the Psalmist, reminds himself to *wait* upon God:

"Guide me in Your truth.
>> Teach me, because You are the God of my salvation.
I will wait for You all day long" (Psalms 25:5).

David's soul looked to God for his salvation, to be delivered from the snares and evils of the world. This shows an inward exercise and a spiritual attendance that persisted not in external forms but through an inward divine aid. And David was truly encouraged by the goodness of God. The Lord continually strengthened him:

> "I waited patiently for Yahweh.
>   He turned to me and heard my cry.
>   He lifted me out of the pit of destruction,
>   out of the sticky mud.
>   He stood me on a rock.
>   He made my feet steady" (Psalms 40:1-2).

Yahweh appeared inwardly to console David's soul, who waited for God's help to deliver him from the temptations and afflictions which were ready to overwhelm him. His God gave him peace and security. David learned to *wait* patiently upon God. David's mind was calm, watchful, and focused upon God's law and Spirit. He felt close to the Lord. David's humble prayer entered heaven and it prevailed. Then deliverance came in God's time, not David's time. David gained strength to overcome all of his troubles. He tells us of "a new song" of praise which was put into his mouth (Psalms 40:3). But it was of God's making, and not his own.

On another occasion, we hear David crying out desperately:

> "A deer thirsts for a stream of water.
>   In the same way, I thirst for You, O God.
> I thirst for God, for the living God.
>   When can I go to meet with Him?" (Psalms 42:1-2)

This goes well beyond formality, and it can be tied to no other lesson. But by this we may see that true worship is an *inward* act. The soul must be touched and raised in its heavenly desires by the heavenly Spirit. True worship is in God's presence. It's not in the temple or with outward sacrifices, but before God—in His presence. The souls of true worshipers must see God (Matt. 5:8). They must appear directly before Him. That's what they were waiting for, panting for, thirsting for. Look how far the majority of "Christendom" has strayed from David's example! It's no wonder that this good man tells us:

> "I wait patiently for God.
> He alone is my hope" (Psalms 62:5).

It is as if he had said: "No one else but God can prepare my heart or supply my needs. It doesn't come from me or the physical worship that I can give Him. Those things are of no value. They can't help me or please Him. So, I wait upon my God for His strength and power to present myself before Him in the manner that will be the most pleasing to Him. He is the One who prepares the sacrifice that will surely be accepted! David says it this way:

> "My soul waits for the Lord to help me
> more than night watchmen wait for the dawn"
> (Psalms 130:6).

Yes, so intently did David wait patiently that he says in another place:

> "I am tired of calling out for help.
> My throat is sore.
> My eyes are strained
> from looking for my God" (Psalms 69:3).

David was not content with saying multitudinous prayers or going through the repetitive motions of a set form of worship. No, he didn't leave the presence of God until he discovered the Lord. That's when he found peace in his soul. Others in spiritual "Israel," the true people of God, found the Lord, too:

"Listen, male slaves depend upon their masters.
And, a female servant depends on her mistress.
In the same way, we depend upon Yahweh, our God,
        until He shows us mercy" (Psalms 123:2).

In another place, David says:

"So, we will wait for Yahweh!
He is our Help, our Shield to protect us" (Psalms 33:20).

And,

"O God, I will thank You forever for what You have done.
        And, I will hope in Your Name (because it is good).
I will worship You publicly among Your godly people"
(Psalms 52:9).

David recommends this advice to others:

"Wait for Yahweh's help.
Be strong and be brave and wait for Yahweh's help" (Psalms 27:14).

This means to wait in faith and patience, and He *will* come to save you!
Again, David wrote:

"Wait on Yahweh and be patient with Him" (Psalms 37:7a).

The Apostle Peter wrote this: "Throw all your worries onto God, because He cares for you" (1 Pet. 5:7). Be content. Wait for Him to help you in your needs. You cannot control how near He is (Philp. 4:5b) to helping those who wait upon Him. "Have faith in God" (Mark 11:22), said Jesus.

Yet again, David bids us:

"Wait on Yahweh and follow Him" (Psalms 37:34).

Why do so few profit from prayer? It is because they are not following God. That's why they can't wait upon Him. David had learned patience by his many hard experiences.

The prophet Isaiah tells us, that, even though the Lord severely punished the people for their waywardness, they had learned to wait upon God (Isa. 26:8). They knew that they had sinned, and that they deserved to be punished by God, but they still wanted to know God:

"Look, our God is doing this!
We have trusted in Him,
and He has come to save us" (Isa. 25:9).

All "worship" which does not originate in faith is fruitless to the worshiper. It is also displeasing to God. The nature of faith is to purify the heart (Acts 15:9b) and give us a victory over the world (1 John 5:4). Isaiah continues:

"So, Yahweh wants to show His mercy to you people.
He wants to rise up and comfort you.
The Always-Present One is a fair God.
And, everyone who waits for His help will be happy"
(Isa. 30:18).

The prophet adds this statement:

"But the people who trust in Yahweh will become strong again.
They will be able to soar, as an eagle in the sky.
They will run without getting tired.

They will walk without becoming weary" (Isa. 40:31).

Isaiah's encouragement is great. Hear him once more:

> "Since ancient times, no one has ever heard of such a God as You.
>   No ear has perceived,
>   no eye has ever seen a God other than You.
>   You help the people who trust You" (Isa. 64:4).

Behold the inward life and the joy of the righteous, the true worshipers, those whose spirits have bowed to the appearance of God's Spirit in them, leaving and forsaking all, and embracing whatever the Spirit has led them to!

In Jeremiah's time, the true worshipers also waited upon God:

> "Do worthless idols have the power to bring rain? No.
>   Does the sky itself have the power to send down showers
>   of rain?
>   No, it is You—Yahweh, our God—who causes such things to
>   happen!
>   You are our only hope!
>   You are the One who caused all these things!" (Jer. 14:22)

And Jeremiah reassures us:

> "The Always-Present One is good to those who put their trust in
>   Him,
>   to the person who looks to God for help" (Lam. 3:25).

The prophet Hosea also exhorts God's people to turn and wait upon God:

"You must return to your God.

You must be loyal to Him.

You must do what is honest.

You must always trust in Him as your God" (Hosea 12:6).

And, the prophet Micah is very zealous and resolute in encouraging us:

"I will look to the Always-Present One for help.

I will wait confidently for the God of my salvation.

My God will listen to me!" (Micah 7:7).

Thus did the children of the Spirit who thirsted after an inward sense of God. The wicked cannot say so, nor those who pray in vain, unless they learn to *wait* upon God. Israel did not wait to hear God's counsel. But we may be sure that it is our duty! God requires it in the Book of Zephaniah:

"So, just wait for Me!"

declares the Always-Present One.

"Some day, I will hold court and be the Judge" (Zeph. 3:8).

O that all who profess the Name of God would so wait, and not attempt to worship without waiting for God. They should feel His stirrings within them to help and prepare them, and to sanctify them. Christ expressly ordered his disciples with this instruction: "Wait here for the Father's promise that you heard me talk about. John immersed people in water, but in a few days *you* will be immersed in the Holy Spirit" (Acts 1:4b-5). He wanted to prepare them for the proclamation of the glorious gospel of Christ to the whole world (Matt. 28:18-20). It was an extraordinary outpouring of the Holy Spirit on the day of Pentecost for an extraordinary work.

TRULY WAITING ON GOD

I WILL CLOSE THIS scriptural doctrine about waiting on God with that great passage in the Gospel of John concerning the pool of Bethzatha. It reads as follows:

"Near the Sheep Gate in Jerusalem there is a pool that is called Bethzatha in the Aramaic language. It has five porches. A crowd of people used to lie around among the porches. Some of them were sick, blind, lame, or crippled.[1] One had been there for 38 years with his sickness. When Jesus saw the man lying there, he knew that the man had been there a long time. Jesus asked him, "Do you want to be well?" The sick man answered Jesus, "Mister, I don't have anyone to put me into the pool when the water stirs. While I am going, someone else goes ahead of me." Jesus said to him, "Get up! Pick up your small bed and walk!" Immediately, the man got well. He picked up his bed and began walking around. (This happened on a Sabbath day.) (John 5:2-9).

That pool in old Jerusalem was for those who had some infirmity of the body. But that fountain could represent all those who are impotent in soul. There was something that moved in the water to render it beneficial. Whatever it was, it blessed somebody with success. Those who got in first got better, but those who weren't ready to get in quick and take advantage of the stirring of the water found no benefit by stepping in. Similarly today, those who are not waiting for the movements of God, but are, by the "devotions" of their own making and timing, rush *ahead* of God (like a horse rushing into battle) cannot hope for success. They are sure to be disappointed in their expectations. Therefore, as they waited then with all patience and attention upon the water's activity, those who wanted and desired to be cured, so do the true worshipers of God today need to wait

---

1   Many late manuscripts have all or part of the following: "waiting for the moving of the water, [4] because an angel of the Lord went down at certain times into the pool and stirred up the waters. The first one into the pool after the waters were stirred up was healed of whatever disease that he had."

and pray for His presence, just as the plants of the field wait for the sun to shine upon them. They shouldn't dare to put up a device of their own or offer an unsanctified request. In the light of Jesus, they were always waiting, not being distracted by any thought which might cause them to miss seeing the waters move. We don't want to call upon God before His timing! And, we don't need "devotionals" in His absence, for they are fruitless and foolish.

> "You come to appear in front of Me.
> But who asked you
> to do all this running in and out of My court
> yards?" (Isa. 1:12)

"Anyone who trusts in it will never be disappointed" (Isa. 28:16).

Those who "worship" God with their own agendas can only end up as the Israelites did. They turn their ear-rings into an engraver's image and are cursed for their painful efforts. They won't fare any better than the gathered sticks (Num. 15:32-36) of the Old Testament:

> "But, look, all of you want to light your own fires, instead.
> You want to make your own light.
> So, go ahead, walk in the light of your own fires!
> Trust your so-called "light" to guide you!
> But, if you do, this is what you will get from Me:
> You will lie down in a place of pain!" (Isa. 50:11)

God told those people that it wasn't going to do them any good. It would only incur judgment from Him. Sorrow and anguish of soul would be their portion. Alas, lots of people today want to pray and pray and pray. They are not waiting for God. They want to be "saint-like" but they're not abiding to do the will of God or suffer for it. Their tongue calls Jesus "Lord"

(Luke 6:46), but not by the Holy Spirit (1 Cor. 12:3). They often name the name of Jesus (Matt. 7:22), yes, even bow their knee to it, but are they free from iniquity? That is an abomination to God!

FOUR NECESSARY THINGS

IN SHORT, THERE ARE four things which are absolutely necessary to worship God the right way:

1. The first is the *sanctification* of the worshiper.
2. The second is the *consecration* of the offering.
3. The third is *praying* for the right thing, as God's Spirit directs.

The Apostle Paul put that beyond dispute: "We don't know how we should pray, but the Spirit helps our weakness. He personally talks to God for us with feelings which our language cannot express" (Rom. 8:26). People unacquainted with the work and the power of the Holy Spirit are ignorant of the mind of God. They could certainly never please Him with their prayers. It's not enough to know what *we* want. We need to learn whether or not something may be sent as a blessing in disguise. The proud ones might need to be disappointed. The greedy might need to lose money. The negligent might need to suffer some punishment. Removing these consequences would not help someone to grow in understanding their salvation.

This vile world knows nothing but carnality. That's the only way they know how to interpret events. They are apt to call "providence" by the wrong names. For instance, they say that afflictions are "judgments," and "miseries" could really be fiery trials which are more precious than gold (1 Pet. 1:6-7). On the other hand, they call the promotions of the world by the name of "honor," and they think that "wealth" is happiness. But the Apostle Paul said, "Loving money is the root of all kinds of evil. Some people want money so badly that they have wandered away from the faith. They have so painfully wounded themselves" (1 Tim. 6:10).

Therefore, what to keep, what to reject, what to want is a difficulty that only God can resolve for the soul. And, since God knows better than we do as to what we need, He is the One who can better tell us what to ask for than we can! Christ exhorted his disciples to avoid long and repetitious prayers (Matt. 6:7-8), telling them that their heavenly Father already knew what they needed before they even asked for it. So, Jesus gave them a simple pattern to pray by:

> "This is the way you should pray:
>   'Our Father in heaven, may Your name always be kept holy.
>   May Your kingdom come.
>   May what You want done be done.
>   May it always be here on earth as it is in heaven.
>   Give us the food we need each day.
>   Forgive us of the sins we have committed,
>   as we forgive everyone who has done wrong to us.
>   Keep us away from temptation.
>   Rescue us from the evil one' " (Matt. 6:9-13).

It was not some fancy, long text for human liturgies. We need to avoid things like that. It is not the request but the frame of the petitioner's spirit. The prayer may seem to be proper, but is it defective? God doesn't need to be told of our wants by us. He is the One who must tell us! Yet He likes to hear it from us, if we but seek Him. Then He will come down to us.

Isaiah reminds us of this with these words:

> "These are the kind of people whom I am pleased with:
>   those who are not proud or stubborn;
>   those who revere Me" (Isa. 66:2).

These are the people with sick hearts and wounded souls. They are hungry, thirsty, weary and carrying "heavy loads" (Matt. 11:28). Such sincerity needs a Helper.

The fourth requirement must also be present. It is *faith*—true faith, a precious faith (2 Pet. 1:1), an honest faith (1 Tim. 1:5), the faith of God's chosen people (Titus 1:1) that purifies hearts (Acts 15:9) and overcomes the world (1 John 5:4).

This is what animates prayer and presses it home. It's like the persistent woman who was mentioned in Luke 18:3-7. She would not be denied! Christ admired her, just as he once remarked to another woman, "O woman, great is your faith!" (Matt. 15:28).

This is of the highest importance on our part. We need to give God the credit. It's not by our power; it is the gift of God (Eph. 2:8-9)! Otherwise, true faith is lost.

James put it this way: "Even if you do ask, you don't receive, because you ask, so that you may use it in an evil way for your own selfish desires" (James 4:3). They seek but they don't find. They knock, but it is not opened for them (Matt. 7:7-8). Why? The case is plain; their requests to God are not mixed with purifying faith, by which they should prevail. When Jacob wrestled with God, Jacob prevailed (Gen. 32:22-32). The truth is, these "spiritual adulterers" (James 4:4) are still in their sins. They are still following the lusts of their hearts and living in worldly pleasure, being strangers to this precious kind of faith. The author of Hebrews wrote: "We were told good news, as they were, but the message they heard didn't help them, because they didn't believe it. (Heb. 4:2). Can the minister preach without faith (Rom. 10:14-15)? No! And neither can anyone purposely pray without faith (Heb. 11:6), especially when we are told: "The person who is right with God by faith will live forever. But if that person moves back, I will not be pleased with him" (Hab. 2:3; Heb. 10:38).

Worship is the supreme act of a person's life!

THE NECESSITY OF FAITH

This explains why Christ rebuked his disciples with his oft-repeated phrase, "O ye of little faith!" (Matt. 6:30; 8:26; 14:31; 16:8). Just one little grain of faith, even though it is as tiny as a mustard seed, if true and right, is able to remove mountains (Matt. 17:20). Paul indicated that there is no temptation so powerful that it cannot be overcome (1 Cor. 10:13). Therefore, those who are captivated by temptations and remain unsupplied in their spiritual needs do not possess this powerful kind of faith. That is the true cause behind their ineffective prayers (James 5:16). It was so necessary that Christ could *not* do miracles where the people did not believe (Mark 6:5). But he performed many wonders in other places because faith opened the way. So, it is hard to say whether it is power by faith or faith by power which works the cure.

Let us call to mind what marvelous things a little clay and spittle can do (John 9:6-7), or just one touch of the hem of Christ's garment (Luke 8:43-48), or a few words out of Jesus' mouth that said: "Do you believe that I can do this?" They said to him, "Yes, Lord" (Matt. 9:28). "Yes, Lord," say the blind, and they see! Jesus said to the ruler of the synagogue: "Don't be afraid! Just believe!" (Mark 5:36). He did, and his dead daughter recovered life. Again, in another place, Jesus says: "All things are possible for the person who believes." Immediately an epileptic boy's father cried out, "I believe! Help me when I don't believe enough!" (Mark 9:23-24) One time Jesus said to another blind man: "Go. You are made well, because you believed." Immediately the man was able to see again. He began to follow Jesus on the road (Mark 10:52). And to another, Jesus said: "Your sins are forgiven. . . . Because you believed, you are forgiven. Go in peace" (Luke 7:48,50). On another occasion, to encourage his disciples to believe, who were admiring how soon Jesus' sentence was executed upon the fruitless fig tree, he tells them: "I am telling you the truth, if you have faith and don't doubt, you will be able to perform this, too! You can even say to this mountain, 'Pick yourself up and throw yourself into the sea!' and it will happen. If you believe, then you will receive everything you ask for in prayer" (Matt. 21:21-22). This one passage convicts "Christendom" of gross infidelity. Why? Because it prays but does not receive any answer from God!

But some may say that it is impossible to receive everything that a person may ask for. It is *not* impossible! The fruits of faith are not impossible for those who truly believe in the God that makes them possible (Matt. 19:26).

But then some will say, "It is impossible to have such faith!" This faithless generation (Matt. 17:17) would excuse their lack of faith by making it impossible to have the faith that they want! But Christ's answer to the infidelity of that age refuted that disbelief: "God can do things which do not seem possible to man. God can do anything!" (Mark 10:27). "It is impossible to please God without faith" (Heb. 11:6), for so the author to the Hebrews taught.

TRUE FAITH

BUT SOME MAY SAY, "What is this kind of faith that is so necessary to worship, and what gives it such acceptance with God and returns that benefit to men?" I say that it is a holy resignation to God and a total confidence in Him backed up by an obedience to His holy requirements. "Faith is the title-deed to the things we hope for. Faith is being sure of things we cannot see" (Heb. 11:1). Such a faith purifies the hearts of those who receive it (Acts 15:9b). The Apostle Paul is a witness that it dwells only within a pure conscience (1 Tim. 3:9). In one place, he couples a pure heart with a good conscience and an honest faith (1 Tim. 1:5). In a later verse, he says, "Hold on to the faith and a good conscience" (1 Tim. 1:19). James joins faith with righteousness (James 2:14-26). And the Apostle John appends faith to a total victory over the world: "Everyone who is a child of God conquers the world. It is our faith which conquers the world" (1 John 5:4).

The heirs of this type of faith are the *true* children of Abraham (John 8:31-43; Rom. 4:12; Gal. 3:6-7). *They* are the ones who are really walking in the steps of Abraham, according to the obedience of faith. That is the only thing that entitles people to be the descendants of Abraham! They live above the world. No man comes to this kind of faith except through a death to "self" by the cross of Christ and through a total dependence upon him and upon God!

Famous are the exploits of this divine gift of faith. Time would fail to recount these adventures. The Scripture's sacred story is filled with them. But let it be known that the saints of old endured all their trials, and overcame all their enemies, and prevailed with God's help, and finished their testimonies, and obtained the reward of the faithful, a crown of righteousness (2 Tim. 4:8), which is the eternal blessedness of the righteous.

PRIDE

CHAPTER 6

The Wrong Kind of Pride

*P*REVIOUSLY, I HAVE ALREADY conscientiously shown how the unlawful "self" wants to be a "Christian" yet an abject stranger to the real cross of Christ. And, I have carefully demonstrated that true worship which is pleasing to God cannot be separated from "carrying the cross." Now, with the Lord's help, I will now attack that other kind of unlawful "self." It occupies most of the attention of the world. This type comes to us in the form of these three major sins—pride, greed, and materialism. All other sins flow from these every day, just as streams originate from their fountains.

You can kill these desires by carrying the true cross in a different way. Ultimately, it's our duty to eventually eradicate these engrained, evil habits in our lives. When we've accomplished this, the happy results of a much-needed reform will begin to show itself in the lives of the followers of Christ. This Man from heaven is perfect (Matt.5:48); we are not. However, we can acquire the traits of repentance, humility, self-control, love, patience, and heavenly-mindedness. These are all "fruits of the Spirit" (Gal. 5:22-23; Eph. 5:9).

THE RISE OF PRIDE

PEOPLE EITHER LOVE GOD or they love themselves. Supreme love must center in one of these two. Those who love God more than anything else are always humbling "self" in deference to God's commands. They love to serve the One who is Lord of all (Acts 10:36). But those who recoil from loving God are only "lovers of themselves" (2 Tim. 3:2). The Apostle Paul rightly classifies all proud, heady, and high-minded people (2 Tim. 3:4) under the category of inordinate self-love. Some angels chose to rebel against God (Luke 10:18; Rev. 12:7-9). Their sad defection started because of their pride and love for themselves. They tried to steal a piece of God's authority over creation. "God punished angels who sinned. He sent them to hell. They were put in chains in the dark. They will be guarded there until the time for judgment" (2 Pet. 2:4). "Some angels did not keep their first position. Instead, they left their home. They have been kept in darkness below in chains forever, until the great Day of Judgment" (Jude 1:6).

It was pride that began mankind's journey of misery. Pride has a very mischievous quality in it. It is commonly recognized by its tragic effects. Every impenitent, human breast carries pride's definition within it. And what is pride? It is simply an excess of self-love. It undervalues others and desires to dominate them. This view causes a lot of trouble in the world.

People can best detect pride by recognizing its four principal forms:

1. The first is one's undue pursuit of human knowledge; the desire to be smarter than others.

2. The second is one's ambitious craving for more power; the desire to be over others.

3. The third is an extreme desire for others to worship them; the desire to be superior to others.

4. The last excess is that of collecting more and more possessions; the desire to have more "things" than others.

AMBITION

AT THE VERY BEGINNING of man's history, it is plain that he had an un-healthy curiosity which led to his plight. This brought about a universal fall from the glory of his original status. Adam was trying to be smarter than God made him. Adam was not satisfied with just knowing his Creator and giving God what was due to Him. Though Adam had a superior intel-lect to and above all the animals of the field, the birds of the air, and the fish of the sea, as well as a God-given dominion to rule over all of God's visible creation, Adam wanted more. Secretly, he wanted to be as "wise" as God. This foolish quest, this unwarranted ambition, caused Adam to be unwor-thy of the blessings that he received from God. Eventually, it drove him and his wife out of Paradise. Instead of being God's chosen caretaker of the whole world, Adam became the most wretched vagabond on the earth!

That was a strange turnaround of roles! Instead of being "wise as gods" (Gen. 3:5), Adam and his wife fell far below the very animals that they were supposed to be in charge of. Ironically, in comparison to the animals, God had already made the first human couple God-like to all other crea-tures. The lamentable consequence of this great mutiny was the exchange of innocence for guilt, and a Paradise for a wilderness. Even worse, in this fallen state, Adam and Eve had gotten another god than the only true and living God. It was Satan, the god of this world (2 Cor. 4:4). He cleverly lured them into a blatant rebellion against God. And how did the Devil do this? He furnished them with a vain knowledge and ruinous "wisdom" through clever deceptions, shifts, evasions, and excuses. Adam and Eve had lost their plainness and sincerity. Their hearts had once been morally up-right. That was the original image in which God had made them (Gen. 1:26). Instead, they became like the crooked, entwining, twisting snake who successfully tempted them, the image of that unrighteous spirit who caused them to lose their perfect happiness.

This Biblical account is not limited to Adam, because all of us "have sinned and we are far away from God's glory" (Rom. 3:23). We are sons of disobedience, "naturally deserving punishment" (Eph. 2:3). Like Adam, all of us have eaten something forbidden. Each one of us have done some things that we shouldn't have done, and left undone some things that we should have done (James 4:17).

Adam and Eve sinned against that divine light of knowledge which God gave to them. They grieved His Holy Spirit (Eph. 4:30). "On the day that you eat of it you will surely die!" (Gen. 2:17). That is, when you do something that you shouldn't do, you will no longer live in God's favor and enjoy the comforts of the peace of His Spirit. In a way, that is a type of "dying" to all those innocent and holy desires which God created in man. Instead, man becomes cold, numb, and insensitive to the love of God and His Holy Spirit, and devoid of power and wisdom, missing the light and joy of God's countenance and the evidence of a good conscience (Acts 23:1; 1 Tim. 1:19) and the approval of God's Holy Spirit.

Yes, that dismal sentence was executed, and fallen Adam no longer enjoyed that daily walk with God. Adam would not experience the love of God working in his soul. Adam became only a shell of a man—puffed up, arrogant, high-minded, impatient, a contradiction! Before Christ came to earth, that was the same attitude found in those apostate Jews. And, it has been the same condition of apostate Christians ever since Christ left!

FALSE KNOWLEDGE

SO, THE KNOWLEDGE OF depraved and unrepentant people is tainted (Rom. 1:20-22). Why? Because it originated from the commission of evil, and it is held within an evil and impure conscience within those who disobey God's laws, and who do those things every day which they shouldn't do. They stand condemned before God's judgment seat (Rom. 2:3; 14:10; 2 Cor. 5:10; Heb. 9:27) among the souls of men. The light of God's presence searches the most hidden things of darkness (1 Cor. 4:5), the most secret thoughts, and concealed inclinations of ungodly men. He knows.

This defiant, human "knowledge" is impure, argumentative, hard to convince; willful, perverse, and persecuting. It is suspicious that somebody might be better at being hateful and abusive. It's quite different from a godly person: "However, the wisdom which comes from God is first pure, then peaceful, gentle, willing to obey, full of mercy and good deeds, without doubts or hypocrisy" (James 3:17).

It was pride that made Cain a killer (Gen. 4:8). He was spiteful, full of envy and wanted revenge. He thought, "Isn't my worship just as good as Abel's!?" Cain may have gone through the motions of an external worship to God. He could have offered things just as well as Abel, but Cain wasn't offering his heart! From the very beginning, God was seeking something more. "By faith, Abel offered God a better sacrifice than Cain did. Abel was a good man, through faith. God was pleased with his gifts" (Heb. 11:4). Well, what was the consequence of this difference? Cain's pride was hurt when he felt rejected by God. Cain couldn't stand to be outdone by his brother. He got mad and resolved to vindicate his rebuffed offering by taking his brother's life. Cain had no regard for natural affection (Rom. 1:31); he savagely stained his hands with his brother's blood by murdering him.

The religion of the apostatized Jews didn't do any better. Having lost the inward life, power, and spirit of the law of Moses, they were puffed up with that "knowledge" (1 Cor. 8:1) that they had. And, in that context, their pretences regarding Abraham, Moses, and the promises of God only served to bolster their incurable pride and cruelty. Later, when God sent many prophets (seers) to them to visit them with His Word, they treated those peaceful messengers as if they were wolves and tigers.

Yes, it is remarkable that the false prophets are always ready to persecute the true prophets. One holy prophet (Isaiah) was sawed in two (Heb. 11:37b), another one was stoned to death (Matt. 23:37), etc. So proud and obstinate is this false Jewish "knowledge" that it impelled holy Stephen to cry out in protest: "You stubborn leaders! Your hearts are not circumcised!

You won't listen to God! You are always against what the Holy Spirit is trying to tell you. Your ancestors did this, and you are just like them! (Acts 7:51).

HYPOCRISY

THE TRUE KNOWLEDGE FROM God came with the joy of angels singing this: "Give glory to God in heaven, and, on earth, let there be peace among those who please God" (Luke 2:14). But the false knowledge received the message with false accusations. They portrayed Christ as an impostor (Matt. 11:18). They wanted "signs" (Matt. 12:38; 16:1; Luke 11:29; John 2:18; 6:30; 1 Cor. 1:22). "Work a miracle!" they said. And when Christ did so, they tried to kill him (John 8:40). They finally accomplished it. But what was their chief motive for doing this? It was because Jesus exposed their hypocrisies (Matt. 15:7; 16:3; 22:18; 23:13,14,15,23,25,27,29), their broad phylacteries (Matt. 23:5), and the "honor" which they craved from men (Luke 11:42). In brief, they give the reason themselves in these words, "If we leave Jesus alone, all the people will believe on him." John 11:47-48 says, "The most important priests and the Pharisees called a meeting. They asked each other, 'What are we going to do? This man is performing many miracles! If we let him go on like this, everyone will believe in him. Then the Romans will come and take us away—our holy place and our nation.'" He's going to take away our credibility with the people, and they will follow *him*, and they'll desert us! Thus, we will lose our power and reputation with all the people."

The truth is, Christ *did* come to demolish their so-called "honor," to overthrow their rabbinical titles, and to bring the people to that inward knowledge of God. The scribes, Pharisees, and Sadducees had abandoned the "knowledge" of God, namely, the Holy Scriptures. Jesus wanted the people to see the deceitfulness of their blind guides (Matt. 23:16,24) who by their vain traditions (Mark 7:1-13) had nullified the righteousness of the law. Those false teachers were no longer reliable expositors of the sacred Scriptures. In reality, they were "the children of the Devil" (1 John 3:10), who was a proud liar and a cruel murderer from the beginning (John 8:44).

Their pride in their false "knowledge" had made them incapable of receiving the simple gospel (Matt. 13:13-15). Christ once thanked his heavenly Father that He had hidden its mysteries from the sophisticated, erudite ones, but He had revealed them to spiritual babies (Matt. 11:25). It was this similar false "wisdom" that also swelled the heads of the Greeks in Athens. They laughed at the preaching of the Apostle Paul, thinking that it was a foolish thing (Acts 17:18,32a). But that highly-educated apostle bitterly reflected later on that so-called "wisdom" which was so much valued by Jews and Greeks: "Where does that leave the "wise" man? Where is the "expert"? Where is the man in the world who can argue so skillfully? God has made this world's "wisdom" look foolish" (1 Cor. 1:20). And Paul gives a good reason for it, "that no flesh should glory in his presence" (1 Cor. 1:29). In other words, so that no person can brag in front of God. Which is to say that God will brand the pride of man as "false knowledge." Man doesn't have anything worth being proud of, unless it's receiving the Holy Bible, the revelation of the Spirit of God. The Apostle goes one step farther. He affirms: "Evil people used their "wisdom," but they could not know the true God. This shows how wise God really is. It pleased God to save people who believe the "silly" message of proclaiming!" (1 Cor. 1:21). Bogus knowledge (philosophy, Col. 2:8) wasn't helping people at all. In fact, it was a hindrance to the true knowledge of God. And in Paul's First Epistle to his beloved Timothy, he concludes: "Timothy, guard what you were given! Turn away from unholy stories, old wives' tales, and the opposition of so-called 'knowledge.' " (1 Tim. 6:20). That was the essence of apostolic times, when the divine grace gave the true knowledge of God to be the guide for Christians.

MAN-MADE TRADITIONS

WELL, WHAT HAS BEEN the success of those generations of people since the apostolic age? Did they do any better than the Jews? Not one bit! Just the opposite. They exceeded the Jews with their pretences of greater "scientific discoveries." Unfortunately, they got further and further away from the true Christian life, even though they had a more excellent pattern than the Jews. God was speaking to them through His beloved Son, who "is the shining brightness of God's glory and the exact picture of God's real being (Heb. 1:3a), the perfection of all meekness and humility. But they seemed addicted to nothing more than an adoration of Christ's name, and a veneration for the memory of his blessed disciples and apostles. So great was their defection from the inner power and life of Christianity in the soul that their respect was little more than formality and pretentious ceremony. Notwithstanding, like the Jews, they were quite zealous in adorning their "Christian" graves, and very careful to carve their images, not only maintaining the pretence as to whose bones a given "saint" might be, but also recommending a thousand other objects as sacred relics. Some of them were purely fabricated. Often they were ridiculous, but surely altogether unchristian. However, as to the great and weighty things (Matt. 23:23) of the Christian law, namely, love, meekness, and self-denial, they were completely absent.. The clergy became high-minded, proud, boasters, without natural affection, aloof, and controversial, always confusing the church with doubtful and dubious questions, filling the people with disputations, strife, and wrangling, driving them into fractured sects. Some of these people were put to death by the Roman church.

O the miserable state of those pretended Christians! Instead of advocating Christ's doctrine of loving enemies (Matt. 5:44) and his apostles' teaching about blessing those who curse them (Rom. 12:14) which they should also teach the people under the notion of Christian zeal, they persecute dissidents. They butcher heretics, instead of offering their own blood as martyrs to be shed for the testimony of Jesus. Thus, that subtle serpent, that crafty evil spirit, the one who tempted Adam out of an innocence state, the one who drew the Jews away from the law of God, has also beguiled the Christians (2 Cor. 11:3). How did Satan do it? By using lying vanities to persuade victims to depart from the Christian law of holiness. Why does he do it? So that they will become slaves to him (John 8:34). The Devil rules in the hearts of "the children of disobedience" (Eph. 5:6; Col. 3:6).

We can clearly see that pride always follows superstition and obstinacy. It was pride that encouraged Adam to seek a higher station than where God had placed him. The same thing happened to the Jews. They were misled to outdo the pattern which was given to them by God through Moses on Mount Sinai. For doctrines, they substituted their own traditions (Matt. 15:3), insomuch that those who refused to conform to them ran the risk of hearing these words: "Crucify! Crucify!" The nominal Christians, succumbing to the same sin of pride, with great superstition and arrogance, have introduced what is obviously ceremonial and worldly practices instead of a spiritual worship and discipline. Such innovations and traditions of men are the fruit of the wisdom that comes from below, not from heaven. Witness their numerous and confused councils and creeds! And notice that they end with these words: "Conform or burn!"

PERSECUTION

IT WAS UNWARRANTED PRIDE that started to pervert the spirituality of Christian worship, causing it to resemble the shadowy religion of the Jews (Heb. 8:5; 10:1), and to look more like the showy worship of the Egyptians than the great plainness and simplicity of the early *ekklesia*, which was not to resemble either this mountain or another in Jerusalem (John 4:21). Now, this same arrogance has spurred them on to maintain their Diana-like idol

(Acts 19:34b) of theirs.[1] It bears no resemblance to the pristine purity in worship and doctrine of the first century church. Nevertheless, these nominal Christians have been led to accept the imposition of their non-apostolic, human traditions. And, bishops of these wayward Christians have quit taking care of Christ's flock (Acts 20:28), and they've become ambitious, greedy, and materialistic. They resemble political demagogues more than they do the humble-spirited and submissive followers of the blessed Jesus. History tells us, with pride and cruelty, with blood and butchery, and with unusual and excruciating tortures, how they have persecuted the holy members of Christ. These true Christians are call "martyrs," but the clergy, like the persecuting Jews, have named them "blasphemers" and "heretics." Nevertheless, they have fulfilled the prophecy of our Lord Jesus Christ, who said, "that they should think they do the gods good service to kill the Christians, his dear followers, which might refer to the persecutions of the idolatrous Gentiles. But, Jesus said, "The time is coming when each person who kills you will think he is offering service to God" (John 16:2b). So, they must be those wolves that the Apostle foretold, the ones that would arise from within the body of Christ (Acts 20:29), after the great "falling away" (2 Thess. 2:3; 1 Tim. 4:1-3) would commence.

I will conclude this section with the following irrefutable assertion: Wherever the clergy has been most entrenched in power and authority, whenever they have had the greatest influence upon political princes and states, there has been an increased number of dissensions, bloodshed, detainments, imprisonments, and exiles. The people were not converted. No, they were so debauched that I don't have enough time to elaborate on the subject. The worship of "Christendom" has now become just a ceremonial, theatrical performance. And the clergy is only bent on obtaining worldly advancements. They're just in it for the money. They want to move onward and upward, getting rich and acquiring longer titles. Their avarice knows no bounds. The apostles foresaw that this would be their trap. This is the ignorance and the misery of irreligion of "Christendom."

1 i.e., images of the Virgin Mary

THE WAY TOWARD RECOVERY

THE ONLY WAY BACK from this terrible defection is to come to a saving knowledge of true religion. We must experience the divine work of God in the soul. We must listen to Him and be obedient. That is what will bring salvation. "The gracious love of God has appeared to save all mankind. It trains us to say no to ungodly ways and worldly desires and to live self-controlled, upright, and godly lives in this world" (Titus 2:11-12). It will get you out of the broad way and put you into the narrow way (Matt. 7:13-14). It will deliver you from your lusts to your duty, from sin to holiness; from Satan to God. You must see yourself for what you really are. You must abhor "self." You must watch and pray (Mark 13:33). You must fast. You must not look at your tempter but at your Preserver. "Bad friends will spoil good habits" (1 Cor. 15:33). Avoid them. Spend lots of time alone meditating. And, be a pure pilgrim in this evil world (Heb. 11:13-14); you are just passing through this life. It's only temporary. That's how you will arrive at the true knowledge of God and Christ. It will bring eternal life to your soul, giving you a well-grounded assurance that emanates from what a person feels and knows within himself. Bad news will not upset you.

POWER

NOW LET US DISCUSS the next most common, prominent, and dangerous effect of this evil that we call "power." Pride wants more and more power. Nothing has been more troublesome and destructive to mankind than this continual craving. I don't need to labor to find evidence of this fact. Most of the wars between nations, the depopulation of kingdoms, the ruination of cities, and the slavery and misery that results are some obvious examples. You yourself can observe how ambitious pride lusts for power. And history consistently records its harmful effects.

SOME EXAMPLES IN THE OLD TESTAMENT

KORAH, DATHAN, AND ABIRAM'S rebellion against Moses is a prime example. They yearned to have his authority. Their not having it was his only "crime." They wanted to be the leaders of that great throng of people. So, they conspired. It was a full-blown mutiny within the camp of Israel. It brought down a remarkable destruction to themselves and to all their unfortunate accomplices (Num. 16:1-35).

Young Absalom rose up against the alleged "tyranny" of his father David, the king (2 Sam. 15:1–18:33). Absalom stood for "the people's rights" (2 Sam. 15:2-6). In his failed coup, Absalom was impatient for power. He was restless. After all, he thought: "I am now the oldest son, the heir. *I* should be king!" But Absalom brought a tragic death upon himself and an extraordinary slaughter upon his whole army. His chief adviser, Ahithophel, committed suicide (2 Sam. 17:23).

King Nebuchadnezzar is another outstanding example of a king's obsession with power. His successes in expanding his empire came rapidly. But it went to his head. He forgot that he did not make himself. He had to learn one lesson—that there was One (namely, God) who was superior to his (Nebuchadnezzar's) power. Nebuchadnezzar built a huge idol of gold, and he forced everybody to bow down to it. If they didn't, they would be burned alive (Dan. 3:1-7). But when Shadrach, Meshach, and Abednego refused to comply (Dan. 3:8-18), it was Nebuchadnezzar who said, "What god will be able to save you from my power!?" (Dan. 3:15). Notwithstanding his convictions, it was the constancy of the convictions of those three excellent young men that proved that king to be so very wrong. Even after Daniel interpreted the king's disturbing dreams, it was not long before the same pride over Nebuchadnezzar's empire filled his heart and his mouth with this haughty question: "Look at Babylon! Did not I build this great city!? It is my royal palace. I built it by my power to show how great I am!" (Dan. 4:30). Nevertheless, while the words were still in Nebuchadnezzar's mouth, a Voice from heaven rebuked the arrogance of his spirit. Then he was driven from society to graze like a wild animal among the beasts of the field for seven long years, until he realized who he really was (Dan. 4:34-37).

OTHER EXAMPLES FROM SECULAR HISTORY

IF WE LOOK INTO the history books of the world, we will find many other instances that human pride does the same thing over and over. I will mention only a few examples for your consideration.

Solon, a famous Greek statesman, organized Athens with his excellent constitution based on laws, but it was the skullduggery of Pisistratus that undermined it.

Alexander the Great, not content with his own kingdom in Macedonia, invaded other lands. The countries that he conquered paid a terrible price in terms of human slaughter and property loss. One man even told Alexander to his face, "You are the greatest pirate in the world!"

It was the same sort of selfish ambition that caused Julius Caesar to betray his masters. He usurped the entire Roman government. The senate had put their army under his command, but he used it against them to put them under his control. Certain freedoms and virtues were cancelled in that republic. Subsequently, it became his empire. After that, it was dangerous to be a Roman senator; they could be banished or executed. Caesar was only interested in being flattered by them. Debauchery flourished.

The vast Turkish Empire is another great proof of my point. They extended their powerful dominion over many lands, thereby causing the shedding of much blood. They simply laid waste major country after country.

And yet, their cruelty has been eclipsed by apostate "Christians." Since the early Middle Ages, their practices are reprehensible. Why? Because they should have known better. Jesus didn't advocate war: "My kingdom does not come from this world. If it did, my servants would be fighting to keep the Jewish leaders from giving me to you. My kingdom is not from here" (John 18:36). But the power-brokers answer to a master that teaches a different doctrine. It may be true that these apostate "Christians" may still call Jesus "Lord" (Luke 6:46), but their own selfishness still reigns. They love power more than anything else! To get it, they will kill, even though they have been instructed by Christ to "turn the other cheek" (Matt. 5:39; Luke 6:29). Jesus taught by example that we are to love and serve one another (John 13:2-17), not kill people. Adding to this tragedy, all "natural affection" (Rom. 1:31; 2 Tim. 3:3) has been sacrificed to the fury of this same grasping for power. How many accounts are there stained with the murder of parents, children, uncles, nephews, etc.?

If we look abroad into some remote parts of the world, we rarely hear of huge wars, but within "Christendom" we rarely hear of peace! A small trifle often becomes the starting point for a major feud. It doesn't matter who gets hurt, as long as the dictators get their way. It doesn't matter how many are killed, or how many are made widows or orphans, or how many lose their estates and livelihoods, or what countries are ruined, or what towns and cities are destroyed, so long as they get what they want! Just 60 years ago, several wars were commenced in England over small disputes, but they ended with great devastation.[2] Consider how often the French, the Spaniards, the Germans, the British, and the Dutch have gone to war.

---

2   The author is referring here to the English Civil War (1642-1651) or perhaps to the turmoil which preceded that general period of time. It was a struggle between the Parliamentarians (or, the Round-heads) and the Royalists (or, the Cavaliers).

EXAMPLES FROM EVERYDAY LIFE

BUT MALEVOLENT ASPIRATIONS NOT only dwell in courts and senates, the raw desire for power seems so natural to people. Daily we see how people are trying so hard to be "great." They all want to get ahead. They seek more exalted titles than they have. They want to look more important and be recognized as important. They desire to surpass their former bosses, stepping on any "friend" who might get in the way. And, they want to settle old scores with their enemies. This causes real Christianity not to be very popular with worldly men. Its kingdom "is not of this world." These ambitious people may say nice things about Christianity and even profess to be "Christians," but they still follow the ways of the world. They are not putting the kingdom of heaven first. Jesus taught: "So, put first God's kingdom and what is right. Then all the things you need will be given to you" (Matt. 6:33). Instead, they want to secure for themselves all the wealth and glory of this world that they can acquire (see Luke 12:16-21). They relegate "salvation" to a sick bed or the most desperate moments of a person's life—if they still believe in the afterlife!

To conclude this section, those who know how to limit their ambitious minds can have great peace of mind. They have learned how to be content (1 Tim. 6:6) with the appointments and bounds of God's providence. Such people are careful not to be "great" (Matt. 20:25-28). True greatness is being humble and doing good to other people.

CHAPTER 7

Humility Vs. Pride

*T*HE THIRD HARMFUL EFFECT of pride is an excessive desire for personal honor and respect. Pride loves power so that it can receive homage. If the power-brokers don't get it from people, then those people will be subjected to pride's anger and/or revenge. Therefore, because this evil trait is so widespread throughout corrupt mankind, it has been the occasion of great animosity and trouble in the world.

In Holy Writ, we have one outstanding instance of what a vengeful, malicious, and proud man is capable of doing when his insatiable appetite for "honor" wasn't gratified. That man was Haman. Mordecai was also one favored by King Xerxes (Ahasuerus), but, because Mordecai (Esther's uncle or cousin) wouldn't bow down to Haman, it almost cost Mordecai his life, as well as the entire Jewish people (Esther 3:1-5)!

Even in our own times, *not* flying a flag or *not* displaying an expected sail, or *not* saluting certain sea-ports or garrisons in a proper way diplomatically, yes, even lesser things, have caused destructive wars among states or between kingdoms! The cost has been very high, both in money and in blood. Likewise, on a personal level, the same sort of thing can happen over precedence of princes and their ambassadors. Duels and several murders have come about because their sense of "honor" was insulted. I myself was once in France. And, about 11 o'clock at night, as I was walking to my hotel, I was attacked by a stranger. He ambushed me with a knife in his hand. Apparently, he demanded "satisfaction" of me because I didn't take notice of him after he tipped his hat to me as a greeting. The truth is, I did *not* see him when he did it. I suppose he would have killed me because he made several attempts at me with that knife! Or, I might have killed him in self-defense. But I disarmed him. (The servant of the Earl of Crawford happened to be passing by and saw this.) Considering the dignity of the nature and the importance of human life, I ask anyone of understanding or conscience, was that whole incident worth the life of a man!? No.

The truth is, because of man's depraved condition in the sight of God, the whole world is just as much out of kilter regarding true "honor" and "respect" as in other things. If people knew what being a true Christian really is, and the genuine "honor" that comes from God, which Jesus teaches, then they would not covet these vanities, much less insist upon them.

Now let me lay out the more specific reasons why I and my religious friends have regarded several worldly customs and definitions of "respect" as simply vain and foolish. Dear reader, I beg you to lay aside all your prejudice and scorn, and with meekness and a discerning mind, to read and to weigh what is being asserted here in our defense. If we are mistaken, then you should pity us and teach us. But don't despise us and abuse us for our simplicity.

CONVICTION

THE FIRST AND MOST pressing motive in our spirits for rejecting these current customs (such as the pulling off of hats, the bowing of the body or genuflecting of the knee, and giving people ostentatious titles in greetings) is what God has revealed to us by His light and Spirit. The so-called "Christian" world has apostatized. That was a great and lamentable defection. We ourselves had to learn the truth. We now see Christ, the One *we* wounded (Rev. 1:7). We too needed to be humbled. The prophet Malachi warned: "No one can live through that time. When He comes, no one can survive. He will be like a refining fire. He will be like a very strong soap" (Mal. 3:2). And, as the Apostle Peter said, "If a good man will barely be saved, then where will the ungodly sinner be?" (1 Peter 4:18 quoting Prov. 11:31). The Apostle Paul said, "We know what the fear of the Lord really means. So, we try to persuade people to live right" (2 Cor. 5:11a). What to do? We should abandon the nature, spirit, lusts, and customs of this wicked world! " 'Come away from them! Be separate!' says the Lord. 'Don't touch what is not pure. Then I will accept you.' " (2 Cor. 6:17 quoting Isa. 52:11). We need to remember what Jesus said: "I tell you, sometimes people talk without thinking. On the Judgment Day they will be held responsible for every word" (Matt. 12:36).

We ourselves were professing religion, but we were grieving God's Holy Spirit (Eph. 4:30). He reproved us in secret for our disobedience. We shuddered to think of continuing "in our old sins" (2 Pet. 1:9). We were afraid of doing good things in the wrong way. Our "heaven" seemed to melt away, and our earth seemed to be removed out of its place. We were at a crossroads, as the apostle said, "we who are confronted by the end of the ages" (1 Cor. 10:11). We feared that we would be destroyed by the breath of his mouth (Rev. 19:21). Jesus did say, "Every plant which was not planted by my heavenly Father will be pulled up by the roots" (Matt. 15:13). He was a swift witness against every evil thought and every unfruitful work; and, blessed be his name, we were not offended by him or by his righteous judgments. Then a tremendous insight came to us: "Every word, thought, and deed was brought to judgment" (Eccl. 12:14), the root was examined (Matt. 3:10; Luke 3:9), and its tendency considered. We learned this one thing: "Don't love the world or the things in the world. If someone loves the world, the Father's love is not in that person" (1 John 2:16). This opened our eyes to "the mystery of iniquity" that is in us (2 Thess. 2:7). And, by knowing that evil leaven (= bad influence) (Matt. 16:6,11,12), and its different evil effects in us, how it had worked, and what it had done, we came to understand the general condition of mankind. We could not allow ourselves to proceed any further with this evil principle in man's depravity. We decided *not* to comply with society. In the presence of an all-seeing and just God, I say that the current "standards" of this world (Col. 2:8,20) have become intolerable to us. They won't lead you to heaven. Those bad seeds grew up overnight (Matt. 13:24-30). They came from "a bitter root" (Heb. 12:15). Only vain, sick minds delighted in them. Those worldly ideas were filled with foolishness and pride!

Even though we knew that people would make fun of us for refusing to comply with these commonly-accepted practices, we were unshakable in our convictions. In fact, that foreknowledge galvanized them. We stand for a high view of man. All men are created equal; each person should be treated with respect. If true "honor" (as defined by God) is a heresy, and our refusal of the homage of taking off our hats, or failing to use the customary titles of man-made titles of "honor," or giving a toast to someone, or playing cards with them, or gambling with them—if all that is "blasphemy," then so be it! We refuse to participate!

SOCIAL ACCEPTANCE

SOME ACCUSE US OF trying to enact strict, outward forms (like a green ribbon)[1] as a badge of our group so that we can become well known. As God is my witness, that is not true. No, these objections are coming from some insensitive men who have speculated what they think we teach. Once people truly understand our simplicity, they are usually touched inwardly and awakened by the mighty power of God. Their consciences bother them, and they easily acquit us. They know that we are not fools or hypocrites.

Some people claim that we are obsessed with tiny details. They think

1   In the 17th century the Green Ribbon Club was one of the earliest associations which often met in London taverns for political purposes. The "green ribbon" was the badge of "The Levellers" (some rural rebels) during the English Civil War. They emphasized popular sovereignty, the legal right to vote, equality before the law, and religious tolerance.

that we are restricting the freedoms of everybody. I answer with meekness, truth, and sobriety. First of all, with God, matters of conscience are *not* insignificant! Next, and this is very important, those who persecute us should not beat us, imprison us, or refuse to give us justice. Often we have been the victims of derision and reproach because of this. This only proves that our convictions are right. Those who oppose us should know that by now. Suffice it to say: "True wisdom is shown to be right by the things it does" (Matt. 11:19). We are only passively eliminating what we believe is vain and "unchristian." We did not set up the forms, but we oppose the forms by omitting them.

CONFRONTATION

THE WORLD IS SO preoccupied with outward, ceremonial things. Throughout the ages, God's wisdom has always challenged conventional, human customs. His prophets always spoke with integrity. The world's standards have always been different from God's standards. The world does not like to acknowledge such things as patience, kindness, sobriety, and moderation. The minds of those who are outside of God's truth stumble when they hear His true revelation. They cannot receive it (1 Cor. 2:12-16). They don't understand its inner beauty. The man who refuses a precious jewel because it is presented in a plain box will never believe that it is valuable. He won't think that it's worth keeping. Therefore, such is a test: Their preconceived rejection only shows where their hearts and affections are hung up, after all of their great pretence to seek more excellent things!

God's people are being mightily tested when they contradict widely-accepted customs which are highly-esteemed in the world. Doing so exposes them to the amazement, scorn, and abuse of the great majority. Nevertheless, there is a hidden treasure in it: It insulates us from reproach. And, it teaches us to detect the false values of the world. We learn how to silently withstand the scorn and opposition of the people around us. We can certainly overcome any injury or reproach with Christian meekness and patience. Our circle of worldly "friends" will get smaller and smaller. They think that we are fools and fanatics. At least, if we are isolated, we won't be tempted to listen to their empty conversations which might actually influence us to sin. Finally, we're in good company with those who fight against the world, the flesh, and the Devil. We're under the banner of Jesus. He knew what it was to be mocked and persecuted. After we have faithfully and humbly suffered with Jesus, we will reign with him in glory. Jesus will glorify his poor, despised, faithful followers with the glory that he had with the Father before the world began (John 17:5). So, that is the first reason why we refuse to practice commonly-accepted gestures of "honor" and "respect."

OBEDIENCE

THE SECOND REASON WHY we refuse to practice your customs in our greetings is because we consider them to be entirely empty and vain. There is nothing of true "honor" and "respect" in them! Since religion and worship have deteriorated into mere form and ceremony, and they have departed from ancient precedents, the original concepts of "honor" and "respect" have been obscured. Scripture and reason are on our side!

In Scripture, we find that the word "honor" is often used in several different ways. First, it is used for obedience, as when God says: "I will honor only those who honor Me. But I will take honor away from those who do not honor Me!" (1 Sam. 2:30). It also signifies the keeping of someone's commands, as in 1 Pet. 2:17: "Honor the Emperor"; that is, "Obey the king." Exo. 20:12 says: "Honor your father and your mother, so that your days may be prolonged in the land which Yahweh your God is giving to you." The Apostle Paul wrote to the Ephesians: "Children, in the Lord, obey your parents, because this is right. The first command with a promise is this: 'You must show respect for your father and mother.' " (Eph. 6:1-2).

Also, Christ uses this word "honor" in the same way when he says: "I am not crazy. I honor my Father, but you don't honor me" (John 8:49). In other words, "I do my Father's will in whatever I do, but you won't listen to me. You reject my counsel, and you won't obey my voice. That was not merely refusing to take one's hat off, or to bow the knee, or other trivial trifles. No, it was blatant disobedience; that is, resisting the one whom God had sent (Jesus Christ), and not believing in him. Jesus charged them with being dishonorable! They said that Jesus was an impostor, but God had ordained him for the salvation of the world since before time began (John 17:24; Eph. 1:4; 1 Pet. 1:20; Rev. 13:18). Even today, there are too many people who "dishonor" Christ! Christ said the same thing back then: "The person who does not honor the Son is not honoring the Father who sent the Son" (John 5:23). They are *not* listening to Christ, and they don't truly worship or obey him. Neither do they hear, worship, or obey God!

In the case of the Roman centurion, whose faith was admired by Christ, he told Jesus: "I, too, am a person under authority and I have soldiers below me whom I command. I can say to one, 'Go!' and he goes. I can say to another, 'Come!' and he comes. Or, if I say to my servant, 'Do this!' he does it" (Luke 7:8). The centurion was their commander. His soldiers respected him because he was a man. He didn't put any stock in silly stuff (like taking one's hat off or bowing the knee) or any effeminate customs of his day. He just gave the orders, and they obeyed him.

HUMILITY

IN THE NEXT PLACE, the word "honor" is used as a trustworthy promotion for doing eminent tasks. So the Psalmist writes when speaking to God: "You have crowned him with glory and honor" (Psalms 8:5). "You gave him honor and majesty" (Psalms 21:5); that is, God has given Christ power over all of his enemies and exalted him to great authority. The wise man so intimates when he says: "Respect for the Always-Present One will teach you wisdom. If you want to be honored, then you must first be humble" (Prov. 15:33). In other words, before advancement is granted, there must be humility. Furthermore, he said: "Just as it does not snow in summer or rain at harvest-time, neither should a foolish person ever be honored" (Prov. 26:1). A fool is not capable of the dignity of trust, employment, or promotion. Such things require virtue, wisdom, integrity, and diligence. These are qualities which fools do not possess. And yet, if the titles of respect which are in use among us were to stand for "marks of honor," then Solomon's proverb would be meaningless. Should silly or wicked men receive that kind of "honor"!? No. Solomon called such men "fools." Those who refuse divine instruction hate to revere the Lord (see Prov. 13:18).

Since virtue and wisdom are practically the same, so folly and wickedness are almost synonymous. When Shechem raped Dinah (Jacob's daughter), it was called "folly" or "a disgraceful thing" (Gen. 34:7). The rebellion and wickedness of the Israelites was called essentially the same thing in the Book of Joshua (Joshua 7:15).

The Psalmist expresses it this way: "My sores stink and have become infected because I was foolish" (Psalms 38:5). He was referring to his own sin. And, "I will listen to what the one true God, Yahweh, says. He has promised peace to His people and to those who are loyal to Him. But let them not go back to foolishness!" (Psalms 85:8).

Solomon says:

"An evil man will be caught in his evil ways.

The ropes of his own sins will tie him up.

He will die because he cannot control himself.

He will be led astray by his own foolishness, which was huge" (Prov. 5:22-23).

Christ puts the word "foolishness" right along with blasphemy, pride, theft, murders, adulteries, wickedness, etc. (Mark 7:21-22). I wanted to add these passages because I wanted to show the difference between the mind of the Holy Spirit and the notion that they used to have about fools who didn't deserve "honor," contrasting what is generally meant by "fools" and "folly" in our time. Then we might better understand the disproportion that now exists between the use of the word "honor", as then understood by the Holy Spirit, and the perception of the same word "honor" by later so-called "Christians."

REPUTATION

THE WORD "HONOR" IS also used to mean "reputation," just as we understand it. Solomon said: "A kind woman gets honor just as cruel men get wealth" (Prov. 11:16). In other words, she keeps her credibility by maintaining her virtue. In another place, Solomon said: "Avoiding fights is the honorable thing for a man to do. But every fool gets involved in quarrels" (Prov. 20:3). Peacemaking will build one's reputation as a wise, moral man.

Christ used the word "honor" this way: "A prophet is not without honor, except in his own country." The context shows that they were offended at Jesus. But Jesus said to them, "A prophet is not accepted in his own hometown or by his own family" (Matt. 13:57). In other words, people believe in a prophet's word everywhere else except where he grew up.

The Apostle Paul wrote to the Thessalonian Christians something to this effect: "Each one of you should know how to control his own body, with holiness and honor" (1 Thess. 4:4); that is, in chastity and sobriety. It doesn't refer to "the latest fashions" at all!

ESTEEM

THERE IS STILL ANOTHER use of the word "honor" in Scripture: Literally, it says: "An elder is worthy of double honor." Or, that could be translated in this manner: "The elders who are good leaders deserve double the pay. This is especially true for those who work hard at proclaiming and teaching" (1 Tim. 5:17). Such a venerable man deserves double the esteem, love, and respect, since he is a holy, merciful, temperate, peaceable, humble leader, especially one who teaches and preaches.

Paul recommended Epaphroditus to the Philippians in this way: "Welcome him in the Lord with great joy. Give honor to men like him" (Philp. 2:29). It was as if Paul had said: "Let them be highly-valued and regarded by you in what they say and teach." This is the truest and most natural, convincing way of giving real respect to a man of God.

In the same way, Christ said this to his disciples, "If you love me, obey my commands" (John 14:15).

Furthermore, the Apostle Paul bids us to "honor" those who are "truly widows" (1 Tim. 5:3,16). Such women with chaste lives and exemplary virtue are honorable.

RESPECT

IN SCRIPTURE, THE WORD "honor" was used between superiors and inferiors. This is clear in the instance of Xerxes (Ahasuerus) speaking to Haman: "What should be done for a man whom the king wants to honor very much?" (Esther 6:6). Later, this was said: "It was a time of happiness, gladness, joy, and honor for the Jews" (Esther 8:16). The Jews escaped the persecution that was about to befall them because of the intervention by Esther and Mordecai. Not only did the Jews enjoy peace, but they also received favor and recognition—"honor."

In this sense, the Apostle Peter advised Christian men "to honor their wives"; that is, to treat them with "honor" (1 Peter 3:7). This means to love, value, cherish, and esteem them for their fidelity and affection toward their husbands, for their tenderness and their taking care of their children, and for their diligence, and the way that they watch out for their families. There was no ceremonial behavior or pretentious titles needed to express that type of "honor."

God "honors" holy men: "So, here is what Yahweh, the God of Israel, says: 'Indeed I promised that your family and your ancestor's family would serve Me forever.' But now Yahweh says this: 'That will never be! I will honor only those who honor Me. But I will take honor away from those who do not honor Me!" (1 Sam. 2:30).

And so we see the word "honor" used every day among people. If important people concern themselves to help the poor, we say, "That great man did me the honor to come and see (or help) me in my need."

HONOR

I WILL CONCLUDE THIS section with one more passage. It is a plain, and pertinent one: "Give honor to everyone. Love the brotherhood" (1 Peter 2:17). Love is above honor, and it is especially reserved for Christian brothers and sisters. But "honor" is the esteem and high regard that you owe to all people, including your inferiors. But why for all people? Because they are the creation of God (Gen. 1:26), and also the most noble part of His creation! They are your own fellow men, too. So, do the right thing. Help people with what you can. Be ready to show any real respect. Smile at them.

And yet, godly David seems to limit the command, "Honor all people":

"O Yahweh, who can stay in Your sanctuary?

Who is allowed to dwell on Your holy mountain?

He must despise vile people,

but he must honor those who revere Yahweh.

He must keep his vows,

no matter what the cost" (Psalms 15:1,4).

Here "honor" is confined and applied to godly persons, but "dishonoring" is interpreted as the duty of the righteous toward the wicked. A mark of their being righteous is dishonoring them or disregarding bad people. To conclude this Scriptural inquiry about the word "honor," I will summarize this subject under three categories: (1) superiors; (2) equals;

and (3) inferiors. There are three principles: "Honor" to superiors is obedience. "Honor" among equals is love. And, "honor" to inferiors is aid.

But how little of all this is to be seen or had in a paltry, empty, tipping of the hat, or bowing, or a cringe, or the use of a high-sounding, flattering title! Let the truth-speaking witness of God in all mankind (that is, the conscience) judge.

The corrupt, proud, and boastful man seeks out these trivial customs, and he becomes angry if he doesn't get to practice them in public or doesn't receive them from others. He doesn't want to listen to me or to others tell him just how "dishonoring" they really are!

That is our second reason as to why we refuse to practice the customary ceremonies of so-called "honor" and "respect." We find no such notion or expression of "honor" and "respect" in the Scriptures of truth recommended to us by the Holy Spirit.

CHEATING

OUR THIRD REASON FOR not complying with such things as popular testimonies of "honor" and "respect" is because such things just don't work. There is in them no obedience to superiors, no love to equals, and no aid to inferiors!

We want everyone to know that we stand for true "honor" and "respect." We do "honor" the king, our parents, our bosses, our government officials, our property owners, one another, and all people who follow God's way. But, we refuse to "honor" these vain and deceitful customs of using meaningless titles, bowing, genuflecting, etc. They are not relevant to real "honor" and "respect."

WORLDLINESS

FOURTHLY, THE VAIN, PROFLIGATE, and worldly people love to flaunt these empty customs. They are the ones who criticize us the most for not practicing them and for our simple lifestyle. From the Holy Scriptures, we already know that these worldly people cannot render true "honor" if they have a dishonorable spirit. They are very adroit at performing all the "politically correct" customs of the day. They are experts at it. But this only proves that these superficial customs are of no real value.

DOING THINGS OUT OF SPITE

FIFTH, I WOULD ALSO like to add hypocrisy and revenge as very common traits of these worldly people. These people care little for others. They practice these worldly customs and niceties of etiquette, but they secretly talk about others behind their back. They are envious, spiteful, hateful, and even plot against one another. Sometimes, when the passions get too strong, outright confrontations and revenge break through these facades. It isn't that way among those who are following the Scriptures! True "honor," which is based on the Scriptures, yields obedience to others or gives preference to others. It never reacts purely out of spite. A true follower of God's Word should love, help, and serve others, treating them with kindness. There should be no deceitfulness, hypocrisy, or revenge whatsoever.

RECENT PRACTICES

OUR SIXTH REASON IS that genuine "honor" existed at the very beginning. But these silly social gestures and most of the fancy titles are of recent

origin. The Scriptures taught "honor" in a better way long before the ballroom dance instructors[2] ever came into vogue! The Bible existed before these silly customs of taking off one's hat, and titles, and debutantes. The original way to express true "honor" is still the best way!

SOCIAL CLASS

SEVENTH, IF SO-CALLED "HONOR" consists of similar, superficial ceremonies, then it would logically follow that those who are the most capable of showing that kind of "honor" would be the ones who perform it the most precisely, according to the latest fashion of the times.

Some believe that man does not have a measure of true "honor" that originates from a just and reasonable principle within himself. Instead, he must acquire this so-called "honor" from skillful, fancy, modern, ballroom dance instructors. Many families pay a great deal of money to have their children learn all of these "honors" (proper etiquette) from someone who is evidently a false teacher of true honor.

This totally excludes the poor country folk, who, though they plow, till, sow, reap, go to market, and are obedient in all things to their judges, landlords, fathers, and bosses, with sincerity and sobriety, rarely are exposed to these ceremonies of high society. Nevertheless, if these simple folk try to perform these rules of proper etiquette, they would be "awkward and ordinary." Their court critics (those hypocrites) would not be impressed; they would laugh at them and make jokes about them. Because of their false notion of "honor," true "honor" has been replaced! It is often said, "He is a man of good manners"; or, "She is a woman of proper behavior." This artificial "fashionable" type of "performance" is ridiculous to the viewer. To the Eastern countries, it's a joke!

2   At that time, upper-class children were carefully taught elaborate courtesies by "dance-masters." Ballroom dancing was held in very high esteem in royal circles. "Dancing-masters" created new dances to obtain the approval of monarchs and their courtiers. The "dance-masters" built entire careers for themselves by teaching their own special style and repertoires. They wielded a considerable amount of influence upon high society.

WEALTH

EIGHTH, REAL "HONOR" CONSISTS not in taking off one's hat, bowing, or having a pretentious title. Money can buy any of those things. Parents send their children for this "special" kind of education in proper etiquette, while they are ignorant of the "honor" that is of God. Their young minds are focused on visible things that perish instead of remembering their Creator in the days of their youth (Eccl. 12:1). They are infatuated with playthings. If they don't comply, they might be disinherited! If parents would truly "honor" God, then they would be better off by helping the poor people with that money instead of spending it on a so-called "education" in formal lessons to enter high society!

BIBLICAL PROHIBITIONS

LASTLY, WE DO NOT regard curious ways of the pulling off of hats, of bowing, or man-made titles to be genuine "honor" because such customs have been prohibited by God, His Son, and His servants in the past. I will now try to prove this fact by several Biblical examples.

MORDECAI AND HAMAN

MY FIRST EXAMPLE IS taken from the story of Mordecai and Haman recorded in the Book of Esther. I think this account will silence the objections which are often made against us. Haman was First Minister of State of the Persian Empire. He was a favorite of King Xerxes (Ahasuerus). The text says that the king set Haman's seat above all the princes that were with him, and all the king's servants bowed down to Haman. The king had commanded that this be done. But it appears that Mordecai did not bow to Haman, nor did he show respect to Haman (Esther 3:1-2). At first, things went badly for Mordecai. Haman commanded that the gallows be prepared for Mordecai's execution. But the rest of the story shows that Haman doomed himself. He ended his pride, along with his life, upon the same gallows (Esther 5:14; 7:9-10; 8:7). Now, speaking as the world speaks, and looking upon Mordecai without knowing how well it actually turned out, wasn't Mordecai very foolish to run such a risk over a mere trifle?

What harm could it have done for Mordecai to bow to Haman, the one whom the king honored!? Wasn't Mordecai despising the king by spurning Haman? And, didn't the king order that respect be shown to Haman? And, aren't we supposed to honor and obey the king? (See 1 Pet. 2:17.) One would have thought that Mordecai might have bowed to Haman for the king's sake, regardless of what Mordecai felt in his heart, and Mordecai would still have come out of the situation in decent shape. Mordecai would have been bowing to the king's authority (compare Rom. 13:1-2), not merely to Haman. Besides, it was just an innocent ceremony.

For the "fine" and "sophisticated" Haman, he was very displeased with Mordecai because he was too plain and simple. On the contrary, Mordecai was an excellent man. He revered God, and he did the right thing. And in this very thing he pleased God, and even the king who had the best reason to be angry at him.

Remember, the king had raised Mordecai to the same level of dignity as Haman—to a greater "honor." At first, the news of the destruction of Mordecai and the whole Jewish race was bad news indeed. But, Mordecai's integrity and humiliation, his serious fasting, and his strong cries to God did prevail. Thus, the people were saved. But the condemned Mordecai ended up being exalted above the princes.

Those who endure faithfully in what they are convinced that God requires of them, though it goes against the grain of the world, and it's not very comfortable for them, *they* will be the ones who receive a rich reward in the end. My brethren, remember the verse about the cup of cold water? (Matt.

10:42). And, "We will receive our harvest of eternal life at the right time. We must never give up!" (Gal. 6:9). Also, call to mind, that the Captain of our salvation, Jesus (Heb. 2:10) did not bow to Satan who tempted him with all the glory of the world: "I will give you all these things, if you will only bow down to worship me" (Matt. 4:9). So should we bow? Oh no! Let us follow the example of our blessed Leader, Jesus Christ.

Before I leave this section, it is proper that I add one more thing. When I was talking with a very prominent bishop (who has since passed away) about this passage of Scripture, I remember how he sought to evade its relevance. Here's how he did it. He said, "Mordecai did not refuse to bow, since it was a testimony of respect to the king's favorite, but Mordecai, being a *figure* and a *type* of Christ, refused to bow because Haman was not Jewish. (Haman should have been bowing to Mordecai instead!)

I replied to the bishop, "Even if I were to grant that Mordecai was a figure of Christ, and that the Jews were a type of God's people (or church), and that, since the Jews were delivered by Mordecai, just as the church is saved by Christ, this still makes the case for me! Why? Because the spiritual circumcision (Col. 2:11-12), that is, the people of Christ, are *not* to receive the fashions and customs of the spiritual uncircumcision or bow down to them. Those people are the children of the world, and those similar practices were condemned long ago in the time of Mordecai. And, they were still condemned in the time of Christ.

On the contrary, this shows expressly that we are supposed to faithfully shun such worldly customs and not to fashion ourselves according to the lifestyle of earthly-minded people. Instead, we must be renewed and changed in our ways (Rom. 12:1-2). We should be just like Mordecai. He didn't bow. So we mustn't bow (Acts 5:29). It doesn't matter what the consequences will be. Mordecai is our example. Like him, we will eventually find favor, if we are faithful.

Therefore, let us all look to Jesus (our Mordecai, the true Israel). He was the one who had power with God. He was the one who would not bow in the hour of temptation (Matt. 26:39,42,44). Christ prevailed mightily, and so he is a Prince forever: "There will be peace in His king-dom forever and ever. His royal power will continue to grow" (Isa. 9:7).

JOB

THE NEXT SCRIPTURAL EXAMPLE which I want to use against these current, secular customs is a passage found in the Book of Job. Here's how it reads:

> "Now, I want to be fair to everyone.
>
> I will not try to flatter anyone.
>
> I don't know how to flatter.
>
> If I did, God, my Maker, would soon take me away!"
>
> (Job 32:21-22).

The question that will arise in these verses is this: What titles are flattering? The answer is obvious. It is those which are empty and fictitious. It's any title which makes a man more than he is, or calling a man something that he is not, just to please him or to exalt him beyond his true name, office, or deserts, merely to gain his favor. Such a man strongly desires titles of "honor" and "respect" such as these:

"most excellent";

"most sacred";

"your grace";

"your lordship";

"most dread majesty";

"right honorable";

"right worshipful";

"may it please your majesty";

"your grace, your lordship";

"your honor, your worship";

and other unnecessary titles and attributes.

These silly titles are calculated only to please and placate poor, proud, vain, and mortal men. Likewise, it is wrong to call a man what he is not, such as "my lord", "my master", etc., and "wise", "just", or "good", when he is none of those things. Why do it? It's only being done to please him. See John 12:42-43.

The same practice existed among the Jews. One time a rich leader asked Jesus, "Good Teacher, what must I do to get eternal life?" (Luke 18:18). It was an accepted salutation or address of "respect" in those times. Here are some current expressions today:

"good, my lord";

"very good, sir";

"good master," (do this or do that).

But what was Christ's answer? How did Christ respond? Luke 18:19 says, "Jesus asked him, 'Why did you call me "good"? Only God is good!' " Jesus rejected the title of "Good Teacher." But he had more of a right to keep it than any other person in the world. So, why did Jesus do this? Because there was One greater than him. Christ could also see that the rich man was addressing it to his manhood, according to the custom of the times, but not to Christ's divinity. That's why Christ refused to receive the title of "Good Teacher." Thus, Jesus was showing us and instructing us that we should *not* give such titles to men as is commonly done today. Only God is due that kind of respect. It is wrong to use these silly titles merely to flatter fallen man.

The plain and simple life was a comfortable one for Jesus. He appeared to be just the son of a lowly carpenter in Nazareth. He openly came to this earth intentionally in order to restore mankind from man's sinful condition to his original innocence and purity at the time of creation (Gen. 1:26-27; 2:7). Therefore, we must be very careful how we address people or give attributes to them which they don't deserve. Jesus said, "I tell you, sometimes people talk without thinking. On the Judgment Day they will be held responsible for every word" (Matt. 12:36).

We sin a great sin if we assign any of God's attributes to man, the creature of His Word, and the work of His hands. He is a jealous God (Exo.

20:5; 34:14; Deut. 4:24; 5:9; 6:15; Josh. 24:19), and will not give His glory (honor) to another! Besides, it is very close to the same sin of the aspiring, fallen angels. They desired to be greater and better than they were made by the great Lord of all. So, to entitle man to a station that is above his standing looks very much like idolatry. (And that was the unpardonable sin under the Law of Moses.) It is hard to comprehend how men and women who profess to be "Christians" could continue to practice such things, much less argue in favor of them! Such things seriously reflects upon their vanity.

It seems that Elihu, one of Job's friends, didn't dare do this. He said, "Lest my Maker would soon take me away" (Job 32:22). He was afraid that God might strike him dead. So, why should we be so bold as to give a man titles that are above him or to give him titles, just to please him!? I cannot yield to that kind of peer pressure. God is the One who should be exalted; man ought to be abased. God is jealous when man is put higher than his own station. Man should keep his proper place, know his true origins, and remember the Rock from whence he came. Everything man has is only borrowed; it is not his own but his Maker's. It is God who brought him forth and who has sustained him. Human beings are prone to forget that. Giving a person flattering titles only adds to the problem instead of telling him truly and plainly what he is. Why should I provoke the displeasure of my Maker? God's anger and jealousy could quickly take me away, bringing my sudden death and untimely end. No, I cannot risk bestowing such titles upon men!

THE PHARISEES

NOT ONLY ARE EXAMPLES of this vain practice of giving undue honor to other men by undeserved titles pointed out in the Old Testament writings, but Christ himself criticizes this foolish custom for Christians. He indicted the Jews, saying that this was a mark of their apostasy: "How can you believe!? You receive honor from one another, and you don't seek the honor that comes from God alone!?" Jesus said to the Pharisees, "You make yourselves look good in front of people, but God knows what is really in your hearts. The things which are very important to people are worthless to God" (Luke 16:15). These faithless men sought worldly "honor," not the heavenly "honor." It isn't something that is difficult to comprehend when we consider that self-love and the desire to obtain "honor" from men is inconsistent with the love and humility of Christ. The Pharisees only sought the good opinion and "respect" of the world (Matt. 6:1-4). So, how could they consider abandoning everything to follow Christ!? His kingdom is *not* of this world (John 18:36). It seemed so counter-intuitive to them. And it is clear that this was the meaning of our Lord Jesus when he told them about the teachers of the law, the Pharisees, and others who wanted undeserved honor and mere status among men. He warned his disciples to beware of these practices.

Jesus spoke these words not about the common people but about the highly-educated doctors, the great men, the men of honor, among the Jews. Jesus said, "They like to have the best seats at the dinners and the most important seats in the synagogues" (Matt. 23:6); that is, the places of the greatest rank and "respect." And, regarding the public salutations, Mark 12:38-39 says, "As he was teaching, he said, 'Watch out for the teachers of the law! They want to walk around wearing clothes which make them look important. They like the greetings of respect which people give them in the marketplaces. They always want the most important seats in the synagogues and the best seats at the dinners.' " Similar salutations of "respect" (such as removing one's hat, and bowing the body in a certain way) are present in our time in the market-places and other public venues. And lastly, says Christ, "They love," to be called by men, Rabbi, Rabbi," one of the most eminent titles among the Jews. The Hebrew word "Rabbi" means "my great one." It is a word that is equivalent to many current titles. It is like these expressions: "your Excellency"; "your Grace"; "your Lordship"; "Right Reverend Father", etc. It is upon these men of breeding and quality that Christ pronounced his condemnation, marking these practices as wrong as well as some of the motives of behind them. But Christ didn't leave it there. He strongly cautioned his disciples about this very point of so-called "honor." He warned them: "You should not be called 'Rabbi,' because there is only one Teacher for you. You are all brothers. On earth, you should not be called 'Father,' because you have only one Father—the heavenly Father. You should not be called, 'Leader' because the Messiah is your only Leader. The most important one among you will be your servant. Every person who acts as though he is important will be made ashamed, but every person who truly humbles himself will be made important" (Matt. 23:8-12). These plain passages carry a severe rebuke to worldly "honor" in general. May God forgive us, if we refuse to listen!

NONCONFORMITY

IN HIS EPISTLE TO the Romans, the Apostle Paul made a weighty and fervent statement that is consistent with the doctrine of Christ above. It was this: "So, brothers, with God's tender feelings, I beg you to offer your bodies as a living, holy, pleasing sacrifice to God. This is true worship from you. Don't act like people of this world. Instead, be changed inside by letting your mind be made new again. Then you can determine what is good, pleasing, and perfect—what God wants" (Rom. 12:1-2). Paul wrote to some people who were in the midst of the ensnaring splendor and self-proclaimed glory of the world. Rome was the seat of Caesar and the Roman Empire. She was the mistress of innovation. Her fashions set the standards for the world, at least in the whole city of Rome. This statement was proverbial: "Cure fueris Romæ, Romano vivito mor"— "When you are in Rome, you must do as Rome does." But the Apostle Paul thought differently. He warned the Christians of that city that they should *not* conform. They were not to follow the vain fashions and customs of their

Roman world. They were to leave those things behind. We should learn from them about our world today.

Then the apostle proceeded to exhort those believers and teach them to live the way that God wanted them to live. He said that they should be entirely transformed and changed from the way that the pagan Romans lived. It is as if Paul had said, "Examine whatever you do and practice it. See if it is right and whether it pleases God. Call every thought, word, and action into judgment (John 3:21). Test whether those things come from God or not (1 Thess. 5:21; 1 John 4:1), so that you "may prove (know), what is that good, and acceptable, and perfect will of God."

BEING SEPARATE

IN ORDER TO VINDICATE ourselves, the next Scriptural authority that we appeal to is a passage from the Apostle Peter in his First Letter which was written to: "the believing strangers throughout the countries of Pontus, Galatia, Cappadocia, Asia, and Bithynia" (1 Pet. 1:1). They were the congregations of Jesus Christ in those parts of the world, gathered by his power and spirit. Peter continued: "So, get your minds ready. Be alert. Put your hope completely upon the gracious love that you will receive when Jesus Christ appears. Like children who always obey, don't be controlled by the evil desires you used to have when you didn't know any better" (1 Peter 1:13-14). Peter means that "honor" is not to be found in the vain fashions and customs of the world, to which you once conformed when you were previously ignorant. Instead, now that you have believed in a more simple and excellent way, you should "be sober" (1 Thess. 5:6,8) and "fervent in spirit" (Rom. 12:11), and "hope to the end" (1 Pet. 1:13). Don't quit. Let them go on with their mocking. As obedient children, endure the constant contradiction of sinners so that you may receive the kindness of God when Jesus Christ is revealed. That's why the Apostle Peter called them "strangers," a figure of speech. They were people who were estranged from the customs of the world. They had a new faith and new manners, which were quite foreign to this world.

The following words prove that Peter used the word "strangers" in a spiritual sense: "God will judge you by the way you lived. You should live your lives with respect for God. You are only here for a short time" (1 Peter 1:17). You should pass the time of your being "strangers" (pilgrims) on earth in fear; not after the fashions of this world. A word in the next chapter (1 Pet. 2:9) explains his meaning further. That is where he tells the believers that they are a "special people," namely, that they were a distinct, singular, and separate people from the rest of the world. They were no longer to shape themselves according to worldly customs.

PARTIALITY

I WILL CONCLUDE MY Scriptural proofs with that memorable passage from the Epistle of James. It was against discrimination in general, after the world's fashion: "My brothers, you are believers in our glorious Lord Jesus Christ. So, don't treat people differently: Suppose someone comes into your congregation and that person is dressed in fancy clothes and is wearing rings of gold. Then suppose a beggar also comes in, wearing ragged old clothes. Do you give special attention to the one who is wearing the fancy clothes? Do you seat him in the best place? Then do you say to the beggar, 'Stand over there!' or 'Sit here near my feet!'? Are you not contradicting yourselves? You have become critics with evil motives!" (James 2:1-4).

They knew they had done wrong: "The royal command is found in Scripture: 'You must love other people the same way you love yourself' (Lev. 19:18). If you obey this command, you are doing fine, but if you treat anyone differently, your deeds are sinful! So, according to the law, you will be judged as wrongdoers" (James 2:8-9).

This passage is so complete that there is nothing left for me to add, or for others to object to. The first thing is this: We are *not* to give special preference to anybody! And the next thing is this: If we do that, then we are committing sin and breaking the law of God. That would be to our own peril.

Perhaps someone will still say, "If this is true, then we would be over-turning all distinctions among men!" If that were the case, I couldn't help it. It's not me who wrote that; it was James. James was the one who must answer for saying it. He is the one who has given us this doctrine for Christians! And yet One greater than James said the same thing to his disciples: Matt. 20:25-27 says: "Jesus called for them and said, 'You know that the rulers of the world lord it over their people. Important men use their authority over them, but you must not think that way. Instead, if one of you wants to be great, that person should be your servant. If one of you wants to be important, he should be your slave." In other words, the one who would rule and seeks to be uppermost will be esteemed as least among you.

For if we read the Scriptures correctly, such an expression as "my lord Adam," as if he were the lord of the world, is *not* to be found in the Bible. Neither is "my lord Noah," as if he were the second lord of the earth. The phrase "my lord Abraham" was not used, though he was the father of the faithful. We don't find titles like "my lord Isaac." or "my lord Jacob," or "my lord Paul" either. And certainly nothing like "your Holiness" or "your Grace" appears in the Holy Bible.

Even among the Gentiles (non-Jews), the people simply wore their own names. There was no ceremonial speech like those which are prac-ticed among so-called "Christians" today. There was nothing like that. Historians won't find expressions like: "my lord Solon," "my lord Phocion," "my lord Plato," "my lord Aristotle," "my lord Scipio," "my lord Fabius," "my lord Cato," or "my lord Cicero." None of these are to be found in any of the Greek or Latin classics. And yet, they were some of the sages and heroes of those great empires. No, their own names were enough to distinguish them from other men, and their virtue and employment in the public service were their titles of honor. This modern vanity had not yet crept in among the Latin writers, even though the most learned and noble one like to quote from them.

CHURCH HISTORY

THE CHURCH FATHERS DID the same thing. They went by own names. They did not have any titles associated with their names. Here is a list of famous writers, philosophers, and theologians who did not need special titles: Polycarp, Ignatius, Irenaeus, Cyprian, Tertullian, Origen, Arnobius, Lactantius, Chrysostom, and Jerome. Some more modern writers are: Damascen, Rabanus, Paschasius, Theophylact, Bernard, Martin Luther, Melanchthon, John Calvin, Theodore Beza, Zwingli, Marlorat, Vossius, Grotius, Dalleus, and Amyralldus. None of them had titles attached to their names. British men include: Gildas, Beda, Alcuinus, Horn, Bracton, Grosteed, Littleton, Cranmer, Ridley, Jewel, Whitaker, and Seldon. Going without a title should not be considered rude or uncivil. Why then is our simplicity so despised and abused? (Often this comes from so-called "Christians"!) Jesus Christ, the one whom they profess to follow, has forbidden these foolish customs. I earnestly beg you who advocate these meaningless ceremonies to seriously consider what I have written and weigh it with an open mind.

CHRISTIAN DUTY

TRUE CHRISTIANS ARE NOT as crude as the world thinks. They also know how to show the proper "respect." But the difference among them lies in the nature of the "respect" that they show and the reasons for it. The world's "respect" is an empty ceremony. There is no soul in it or substance to it. But the true Christian's "respect" is a solid thing, whether it is by obedience to superiors, or as love to equals, or as aid to inferiors. Next, their reasons and motives for showing true "honor" and "respect" are far removed from the ways of the world. The fine apparel, the vacuous titles, and big money is what motivates this world. Those are the kinds of things that the children of this world worship. But the Christian's inducement lies in his duty to God.

We will easily grant that our definition of "honor" is more hidden. It may not be discernible to secular men nor appreciated by them. Our plainness seems odd, uncouth, and hard to accept. Well, so does true Christianity for the same reasons. It is *not* palatable. It would not be so hard to discern right from wrong if the pagan spirit had not prevailed so long under the name of "Christianity."

O that Christians would look upon themselves through the lens of righteousness! They should know what rings true and gives them a precise knowledge of themselves! Let them examine what is in them, and about them, what agrees with Christ's true doctrine and his life! Then they could quickly resolve whether they are real Christians, or if they are christened heathens who are merely using the name of "Christians"!

CHAPTER 8

The Characteristics of Pride

WHAT CAUSES PEOPLE TO be so obsessed with their own affairs? It's selfish pride. They think they simply must have the very best stately furniture and the most fashionable, expensive clothes. All this helps to comprise that "pride of life" that the Apostle John tells us about. It is not of the Father but of the world: "These are the evil things in the world: wanting sinful things to please our bodies; wanting the things that we see; being too proud of the things that we have. None of those things come from the Father; each one of them comes from the world" (1 John 2:16).

God accused the haughty women of Jerusalem of this same sin (Isa. 3:16). He also charged the proud prince of Tyre and its people with having a similar arrogant attitude (Ezek. 28:1-19). Today are we guilty of the same thing? What happened to those ancient people because of it?

It is quite obvious that people are generally proud of themselves, and this causes a lot of trouble. This is especially true if they claim to be of noble blood or their faces are pretty. "Blood" has caused many quarrels among men. And, "beauty" has been at the bottom of the dissension among many women, as well as among men who are titillated by a gorgeous face.

So many commotions have resulted because of the so-called "nobility" in the world: "How far back can your family name be traced?" "How famous was your father or mother?" "Who was your great grandfather or great grandmother?" "Who has the best lineage?" "What clan did you come from?" "What coat of arms do you have?" etc. Of all the foolish things that people do, I can't think of anything that has less logic behind it than this sort of thing!

VIRTUE IS BETTER

WHAT DIFFERENCE DOES IT make as to who your ancestors were (Matt. 3:9)? It is one's own virtue that elevates a person, or one's own sins that lower him. An ancestor's character in the distant past is no excuse for a man's sinful actions today. Virtue is not inherited. I am neither better nor worse in God's ledger for my forefather's behavior. And, he won't be judged for my behavior, either (Deut. 24:16; Ezekiel 18:20).

To be descended from wealthy people does not fill anybody's head with brains or his heart with truth. These qualities come from a higher source. It is unconscionable pride for a man of wealth and position to despise another person who happens to have a lesser standing in the world. The latter man may have merit, whereas the former man possesses only the effects of an ancestor's merit. One man may be considered "great" because of his forefather, but the other man might be "great" by his own merits. So, of the two, which is the better man?

But the proud nobleman might say: "It has not been a good world since we've had so many presumptuous 'gentlemen' who are trying to break into our high society!" But what could others have said about that same man's ancestor when he first started to move up in the world!? It had to start somewhere. All men, all families, all states, and all kingdoms have had their humble beginnings. Families are not "noble" just by being old families, but by being virtuous.

How strange it is that some people should be more "noble" than the ancestor from whom they received their nobility! That's absurd. So, the upstart is the true nobleman because he got nobility through his virtue. The only ones who are entitled to real "honor" are those who emulate true virtue. The rest may perpetuate a man's name from his blood, but that is all they can do. Blood and name always go together, but let genuine nobility and virtue keep company because they are the nearest of kin.

God neither likes nor dislikes by heredity. He doesn't concern Himself with what people were, but He does care about what they are. He doesn't remember the righteousness of any man who abandons His righteousness. "A righteous person might stop doing good. He might do wrong and die because of it. If that is the case, he will die, because he did wrong" (Ezek. 18:26). How much less would He remember an unrighteous descendant for the righteousness of his ancestor!

But, if these men of noble blood like to think of themselves as those who revere God and His Holy Scriptures, then they might learn something from this: "God started with one man. He made all the different people in the world to live everywhere. God decided exactly when and where they must live" (Acts 17:26). So, we all descended from one father and one mother—Adam and Eve. Could you have done it any better? After that, we must consider Noah, who was the second planter of the human race. Nobody could brag about descending from Noah because we all came from him. So, how are you better than anybody else?

It should suffice us to say that men of "noble" blood, without their gear and trappings, without their feathers and finery, have no more marks of "honor" stamped on them by nature than their "less noble" neighbors. They should be able to see that for themselves!

Frankly, they will tell us themselves that they feel all the same passions in their blood that make them like other men. It doesn't seem to matter what kind of "blood" that a man has, we are all sinners (Rom. 3:23). The debauchery that now rages among too many people of high society proves this point.

TRUE GREATNESS

WE ARE NOT REJECTING the true "gentleman," only humbling him. What I am writing now only shows to everyone where true "nobility" dwells, so that all may achieve it through virtue and goodness. But for all this, I must admit that today's "gentleman" has a great advantage. And, I can see why he prefers his high position. I grant that the status of our great men is much to be preferred over the ranks of our humbler people.

First, great men have more power to do good. And, if their hearts are equal to their ability, they can be a blessing to the people of any country. Second, the eyes of the people are usually directed toward them. And, if they will be kind, just, and hopeful, the people will love and serve them. Third, they are not under the same pressures of the lower classes. Consequently, they have more servants, more leisure time, and more opportunities to explore their interests by reading books and exchanging ideas. Fourth, they have ample time to observe the affairs of other nations, to travel abroad, and to study the laws, customs and interests of other countries, and then to bring back home whatever is worthy of replicating.

So, there is an easier way for great men to obtain "honor." And, those who love a good reputation will embrace the best means to get it. But, too often, some great men fail to give God the glory for their prosperity. Instead, they try to live without God in this world, fulfilling all of its lusts. Sometimes God's hand brings poverty or even death to these great men, and He raises up other men (more virtuous than they) to take over their former positions.

However, I must admit that, among people of high social standing, there have been some of extraordinary virtue, whose families are very proud of the good things they've accomplished. And, some of their descendants have naturally tried to keep up their reputations (for their own sake).

If there is any advantage to this kind of ancestry, it is not from "noble" blood, but from education. Blood has no intelligence in it, and it is often spurious and uncertain. But education wields a mighty influence upon the affections and actions of people. The ancient nobles and gentry of the British Empire did excel in this regard. Would that we imitate the strict and virtuous discipline of their ancestors, when men were honored for their own achievements, and when nothing exposed a man more to shame than being born into nobility with no virtue to go along with it.

But I have a higher reason to share my beliefs; it is the glorious gospel of Jesus Christ. We should be seeking the "honor" that it has brought to all who follow it, to all the true disciples of it who are indeed the followers of God's Lamb who takes away the sin of the world (John 1:29). Receive with meekness His gracious Word (James 1:21) into your hearts which subdues the world's lusts and leads us in the holy way to happiness. Here are jewels that no carnal eye has seen, nor ear has heard, nor heart has perceived (1 Cor. 2:9). But these things are revealed to humble converts by His Spirit (1 Cor. 2:10). Remember, you are only creatures (Gen. 9:12,15,16; Mark 16:15). You must all die and afterward be judged (Heb. 9:27).

HIGH CLASS PRIDE

PERSONAL PRIDE DOES NOT end with noble blood. It leads folks to have too fond a value of themselves (whether they are noble or ignoble), especially if they have any pretence for physique or beauty. Some are so taken with themselves that it would seem that nothing else deserved their attention. They don't care what other people think of them. Their folly would diminish somewhat if they could spare just half their time to think about God and what's going to happen to them eternally. Instead, they spend all their time in washing, perfuming, painting, patching, and dressing their bodies. They are very precise and artificial in these things, and they spare no expense to "improve" themselves.

But what worsens the wrong is that all the money that supports the pride of just one person could comfortably supply the needs of ten people! (The pride of a nation can be seen in the face of its poor people!) But what is all this primping for? Only to be admired, to attract romance, or to command the eyes and affections of beholders.

These rich people are so obsessed with this. They are hard to please. Nothing is good enough for them. Or, fine enough, or fashionable enough. The sun itself must not shine upon them; it might give them a tan. The wind must not blow upon them for fear that it might mess up their hair. O impious nicety! Yet while they value themselves above all else, they make themselves the slaves of their own pride. They worship their own shape, features, and complexion.

Too often the purpose of all this is to excite unlawful love. (I call it lust.) They are trying to lure one another into an evil situation. This is bad for single persons because it awakens unchaste sexual desires. It lays no foundation for solid and lasting marriage unions.

But the sin is worse among married people. They only have to please one another. But all this coquettish flirting, this gaiety and vanity of youth, is a tell-tale sign that things are not going well at home. It looks more like dressing up to go shopping. It causes sad effects within families: discontentment, separations, poisonings, duels, and infamous murders. How fatal it has been to the sobriety, virtue, peace, and health of families in the British kingdom.

OLD AND UGLY

BUT OF ALL CREATURES, this sort of pride is the least becoming in the old and the ugly people. The old are only proud of what they once had. Their pride has outlived their beauty. When they should be repenting, they are doing things that need to be repented of!

But the ugly ones are even worse. They are proud of what they never had or never could have. Yes, their bodies seem as if they were given to them for a constant humiliation to their minds. To be proud of an ugly body is loving pride for pride's sake! They dote on themselves all the time. They don't see right with their eyes because of the partiality of their minds. This self-love is blind indeed! But spending all that money on something that can't be fixed is sheer madness. Especially if they consider the fact that they look uglier for the things which they think are beautiful. Thus, they draw more attention to their deformity!

But in the follies of such individuals we have a specimen of man's lapse from his original created image (Gen. 1:26-27). As Jesus said, all this sin comes from within (Matt. 15:10-20). Men and women disregard the Word of their Creator in their hearts (Deut. 30:14; Rom. 10:8). It exposes pride and teaches humility, self-abasement, and guides the mind to the true object of "honor," namely, to worship God.

Poor mortals! They are but living dirt, made of what they walk on! With all of their pride, they cannot insulate themselves from the spoil of sickness, much less from the stroke of death! If people only considered the brevity of all visible things, the evil of man's life, the certainty of his departure (= death), and the inevitability of eternal judgment, then maybe they would bring their deeds to Christ's light in their hearts (John 3:20-21). Then they would see if their deeds were done for God or not.

TRUE BEAUTY

THE APOSTLE PETER WROTE: "Your beauty must not be the outer beauty of fancy hairdos, wearing gold jewelry, or expensive clothes. Instead, it should be the hidden personality of the heart with a gentle and quiet spirit that lasts and lasts. This is very valuable before God" (1 Pet. 3:3-4). Are you shapely, comely, or beautiful? Or, are you the opposite? In either case, you should admire that Power that made you so (see John 9:3). You should live in harmony in this life, and let the beauty of your body teach you to beautify your mind with holiness. You are the ornament of the beloved one of God. Are you ugly or deformed? Praise that Goodness that did not make you a beast! And with the grace that is given to you, learn to adorn your soul with enduring beauty. And if your soul excels, your body will only show off the luster of your mind.

Nothing but sin is ugly in God's sight. Those people are beautiful to Him who commune with their own hearts and do not sin. In the light of Jesus, the beautiful ones watch over the inclinations of their own souls, and they suppress every incipient evil (James 1:14-15). They love the yoke of Christ (Matt. 11:28-30) and the cross of Christ, and they are daily (Luke 9:23) crucified by it to the world (Gal. 2:19-20; 6:14). But they live to God in that life which outlives all the fading satisfactions of this life.

WHAT IS A PROUD MAN LIKE?

TO CONCLUDE THIS LARGE section about pride, let us now study the nature of a proud man. A proud man is a type of glutton; he's full of himself. He can never get enough of his own admiration. With him, nothing else but himself is worthy of his love and care. He's the slave of his own will. To him, that's fine, because that is all he can find in his heart to permit. It's as if he was made only for himself. Rather, he is his own creation! Since he despises mankind, he cannot consider anyone to be his equal. By definition, he cannot love God because he would have to acknowledge that there *is* a Superior Being who is above himself. And, the proud man's existence cannot depend upon another.

This man is mighty proud of the "honor" of his ancestors, but not of the virtue that brought that honor to them. He wouldn't trouble himself to emulate them. This proud man can tell you all about his pedigree, his antiquity, his estate, and what matches. But he forgets one thing—they are all gone! And, he doesn't want to think about his own demise!

HE IS OVERBEARING

HOW TROUBLESOME IT IS to be around such a man! He's always trying to control everybody else. And if you don't yield, he'll be insolent and pick a fight with you. He's really a cruel coward. He feels no pity for the miseries of other people. After all, it's not *his* problem. Is it a sin to be sensitive? Since someone else's suffering is not in the proud man's best interests, he looks no further. He won't disturb his thoughts with other men's "unhappiness." He is content to think that they must deserve their suffering. So, instead of helping them, he coarsely scolds them about the cause of their troubles. With him, compassion is a useless term. And, humility and meekness are despicable to him.

HE IS A BAD MAN

THIS PROUD MAN MAKES for a bad child, a bad worker, and a bad citizen. All day long, he bad-mouths his parents, his employer, and the government. He won't submit to anybody. He thinks he's too smart to receive directions from anyone. He says, "I'm too old to change!" He acts as if it were a slavish thing for him to obey. "Everybody is free to do what they want!" he says. So, he shirks his duty, and he undermines all authority.

If he is a husband, a father, or a boss, no one can stand to be around him. He is so testy that it's a real pain to live with him. You can never please him, no matter how much you try to help him. Any minor defect in his clothes, his diet, or his accommodations will thoroughly upset him, especially if he thinks that he's not receiving the proper "respect" that he's looking for. On one hand, he learns to condemn duty. But on the other hand, he turns love into fear, just the opposite of what the Apostle John wrote about: "Love does not contain fear; perfect love pushes out fear.

Love has not been perfected in the person who still has fear; he is afraid of being punished" (1 John 4:8). Instead, the proud man makes his wife his "servant," and he turns his children into "slaves." Thus, pure pride destroys the nature of all relationships.

HE IS UNAPPROACHABLE

THE PROUD MAN ALSO makes a bad neighbor. He is an enemy to hospitality. He despises receiving kindness, because he won't show any human kindness. He doesn't think he needs kindness. Why? Because it makes him look "too equal." His haughty disposition won't allow him to fraternize with ordinary people; they are beneath him. He brooks no rivals, yet he is jealous of everyone. He won't give any praise to others. To him, nothing is praiseworthy. For him to admit that might upstage or lessen him. He can't wish that others do well. He maliciously misnames their acts of virtues, whereas he ought to be imitating them. But he won't give them any credit for their goodness. Instead, he looks for any small excuse to run them down. Of all creatures, the proud man is a most jealous, sullen, and spiteful man. All he wants to do is to get even with people. He never forgives an injury to his person!

HE'S NOT FRIENDLY

BUT THAT'S NOT ALL, a proud man can never be a friend to anybody. You can always count on his personal ambition to be bribed by fame and the possibility of advancement. He'll step on anyone to get to the top. He'll betray "friendship" in a minute.

You can't talk to him about anything. You can't teach him anything. He refuses to take any advice, much less be rebuked or contradicted. And he's much too greedy to share things with anyone. He has no friends. A real friendship requires some give-and-take, but he can't permit anyone to get that close to him. He is much too high, stiff, and touchy. He truly condemns the essence of friendship. Such a thing would be unduly intimate, much too familiar. He'd have to humble himself. His mighty soul desires to know nothing except himself. He wants to have his servants to stock the world. He values other men as we do cattle. They exist only to serve him!

HE IS DANGEROUS

A PROUD MAN WHO is in power is a real problem. His pride is all the more dangerous because of his high position. His pride can easily escalate into tyranny. He would reign alone, and even live alone, rather than have any competition. He won't allow reason to curtail his power nor the rules of law to limit it. If anybody complains, either he claims to do no wrong or he calls that complaint "rebellion." Men of this temperament would have nothing they do thought to be "wrong." A despot cannot permit a dissenting view (even though it might be true) because that would imply that he had made a mistake. (It's always a matter of state to deny that.) No, he would rather choose to perish obstinately than to acknowledge his error. Indeed, destruction is all that proud, powerful men bequeath to the world for all the miseries that they caused. Sooner or later, they follow some emotional whim, and they are almost always destroyed by that. After others have all been dragged down by these dictators, this is the ruination that unbridled pride brings upon proud men.

HE'S A HYPOCRITE

ABOVE ALL THINGS, PRIDE is intolerable in men who pretend to be religious, especially ministers. Pride and religion are names for two of the greatest contradictions. I am not speaking about any particular religious group or person. I'm only touching upon the worst of all of them.

What does pride have to do with religion!? Religion is supposed to be rebuking pride! Or, what does selfish ambition have to do with ministers whose very office is supposed to exemplify humility!? There are too many ministers who are proud of that title "Minister," as well as their exalted position. The word "minister" means "servant," a term which should remind them of the concept of self-denial. But these professional ministers use their office as beggars do. They employ the name of God and Christ only for financial gain. And, they use their official position to advance themselves in the world politically.

But how could they do this!? They're supposed to be ministers of the One who said: "My kingdom does not come from this world. If it did, my servants would be fighting to keep the Jewish leaders from giving me to you. My kingdom is not from here" (John 18:36). But, of all men, who are more conceited than these men? If anyone raises an objection to them, they become even more arrogant and angry. You would think *that* was their calling. If you try to advise one of them, he'll scorn you. If you reprimand him, he's almost ready to excommunicate you! He says, "*I* am a minister and an elder . . . ," attempting to escape the reach of a proper reproof. But in so doing, he only exposes himself more to censure. It is much worse for a minister to do wrong than a layman.

Because of his office, he considers himself exempt. To him it is unthinkable that he could be rebuked or instructed by a layman. (Compare John 7:49.) How could that be, from a man who is younger in age, one with an inferior education and ability!? In no way will the minister allow this. He would have us believe that his ministerial prerogative has placed him out of the range of popular disapproval (and possible impeachment). He thinks that he is not subject to judgments from commoners.

Any valid questions about religion he calls "schism" (1 Cor. 12:25), and the questioner is a "heretic." Everyone must do as the minister says: "It is not for you to pry so curiously into the mysteries of religion. There has never been a good day since laymen began to meddle so much with the minister's position!" He does not been consider that the opposite is more true. Poor man! There have not many good days since ministers meddled so much in laymen's business! Ministers often forget that they are not the personification of the church and the flock of God but only the servants of it.

Remember the words of Christ, "Let him that would be greatest be your servant." Jesus taught that we must not think the most powerful ones are the greatest ones. He said, "Instead, if one of you wants to be great, that person should be your servant" (Matt. 20:26).

There is only one place to be found in the Holy Scripture where the Latin word *Clerus* (Greek: *kleros*) can properly be applied to the church, but ministers have applied it to themselves. That's how they derived the phrase "the clergy" from the word. It really means "the heritage" of God; it's the people, not the minister. The Apostle Peter exhorted the true ministers of the gospel not to be lords over God's heritage (*kleros*); the church leaders were not to feed themselves for dishonest gain. "So, I beg the elders among you to shepherd God's flock among you. Watch over them as God wants you to, not because you have to. Don't be in it for the money, but be eager. Don't act like lords over the people. Instead, be examples for the flock" (1 Peter 5:2-3). Peter foresaw the pride and avarice which would arise among some ministers. He knew that they would be tempted by the love of money, "which is the root of all kinds of evil" (1 Tim. 6:10). In making themselves that "heritage," these renegade ministers have disinherited the people. All they want to do is to dominate unsuspecting sheep!

They are getting the people's money for nothing! An example of this is given to us in the Book of Isaiah. God Himself is complaining about it there:

"But now, those leaders are drunk with wine.
Because of drinking so much liquor,
they can't even walk a straight line.
Their priests and their prophets are drunk with liquor.

They are filled with wine.
Because of drinking so much liquor,
they can't even walk a straight line.
The so-called 'prophets' are drunk
when they see their so-called 'visions.'
The so-called 'judges' stumble
when they render their legal decisions" (Isa. 28:7).

When the so-called "leaders" are corrupt, the people despise them.

DEATH IS INEVITABLE

BUT, ALAS, WHEN ALL is said and done, what folly there is in pride! It cannot add one cubit to any man's stature. Jesus said, "None of you can grow 18 inches taller by worrying about it" (Matthew 6:27). What sufferings can pride stop? What disappointments can it cure? What harm can pride prevent? Pride does not deliver one from death. Sickness disfigures, pain is still excruciating, and death ends the proud man's fabric. Six feet of cold earth limits his big thoughts. The prideful man who thought that no place was the proper accommodation for him must at last reside within the narrow limits of a little, dark cave (crypt)! And he who thought that nothing was good enough for him will soon become the entertainment of the lowest of all creatures—worms!

Thus, pride and pomp come to the same end. But there'll be this difference—there is less pity from the living and more pain to the dying. The proud man's ancestry cannot secure him from death, nor his reputation from judgment. Titles of honor will vanish at this inevitable extremity that we call death. And no power or wealth, and no distance or respect, can rescue him or insure him from death. Eccl. 11:3 says,

"If clouds are full of rain, then they pour out water on the earth.
A tree might fall toward the south or toward the north,

but, wherever it falls, it will lay.
And as death leaves men, judgment finds them."

THE WAY OUT

WHAT CAN CURE THIS falling away (apostasy) from the ancient standard of meekness, humility, and piety found in pure Christianity of the first century? Nothing but a sincere, inward examination of one's soul by the testimony of the holy light and spirit of Jesus. We need to be like the Bereans: "They were very happy to listen to the things which Paul and Silas said. They wanted to know whether these things were true or not. They studied the Scriptures every day" (Acts 17:11).

Long ago, this was Jesus' complaint: "This is the verdict: Light has come into the world, but people loved darkness more than they loved light because the things which they were doing were evil" (John 3:19).

If you would be a child of God and a believer in Christ, you must be a child of Light (John 1:9). You must examine your deeds by that holy lamp which is within your soul. It's the candle of the Lord that shows you your pride and arrogance, and it reproves your delight in the vain fashions of this world. True religion is supposed to be a denial of self. True religion is a firm bond of the soul to holiness. And, the result of holiness is happiness because by it people come to see their Lord. "The pure in heart," says Jesus, "will see God" (Matt. 5:8). Once someone bears Christ's yoke, he won't be carried away by the Devil's allurements. Instead, he will find infinite joy in his watchfulness and obedience.

If people truly loved the cross of Christ, his precepts, and his doctrine, then they would cross their own wills. Their stubborn will is what causes them to break Christ's holy will and to lose souls. They start to do the Devil's bidding, instead. If Adam had minded that holy light in Paradise instead of going for the serpent's bait, if Adam had fixed his mind upon his Creator, the Rewarder of fidelity, then he would have seen the true colors of the snare of the enemy and resisted Satan. Do not delight in what is forbidden. If you don't want to be captivated by it, then don't even look at it! Don't incur the guilt of the sins of so-called "knowledge" upon your own soul (Gen. 3:5). Didn't Christ submit his will to his Father's (Matt. 26:39) for the joy that was set before Him? He endured the shame of flogging and his execution (Heb. 12:2). You should also submit your will to Christ's holy law and light in your heart for the reward that he sets in front of you—eternal life.

All want to rejoice with Jesus, but few will suffer with him (2 Tim. 2:12), or for him. Many join him at his table, but not many in his fasting (Matt. 4:2). They follow the loaves, like the 5,000 who were fed by the Lord. They exclaimed, "Lord, always give us this food!" (John 6:34). But Jesus answered them, "I am telling you the truth: You are looking for me, not because of the miracles, but because you ate the food and were filled!" (John 6:26). They leave the cup of his agony (Matt. 20:22; 26:39,42) behind. It's too bitter; they don't want to drink that! Many praise Jesus' miracles, but they are offended at the dishonor of his cross. For your salvation, you must humble yourself for the love of Jesus, and you must be content to be of "no reputation" (Philp. 2:7), so that you may follow him, not in a carnal, formal way of vain man's tradition (Matt. 15:7-9), but as the Holy Spirit, dictates—"in a new and living way" (Heb. 10:19-20). This is the way which Jesus has consecrated (John 14:6). It will bring all who walk in it to the eternal rest of God. Jesus himself has entered therein, and he is the only holy, blessed Redeemer.

GREED

CHAPTER 9

Covetousness

$\mathcal{J}$ HAVE NOW COME TO the second part of this discourse. It's about avarice. Another word for that is greed. This sin has reached epidemic proportions. It's like a raging, all-consuming "disease" in the world, along with all of its attendant problems. It can make people so miserable. It's very closely related to the preceding sin that we've already discussed thoroughly—pride. It's a fact that greed and pride are seldom apart. Generosity is almost as repugnant to the proud as it is to greedy people.

I will define "covetousness" in this manner: Pure and simple, it's human greed. Greed is the love of riches, and it can keep you out of heaven! Listen to the Apostle Paul: "You can be sure of this one thing: no sexual sinner, no immoral or greedy person (He is the same as one who worships a false god.) will have a share in the kingdom of Christ and God" (Eph. 5:5). He also said that the love of money is the root of all evil: "But the people who want to be rich fall into temptation, a trap, and many foolish desires that hurt them. These things drown people in ruin and destruction. Loving money is the root of all kinds of evil. Some people want money so badly that they have wandered away from the faith. They have so painfully wounded themselves" (1 Tim. 6:9-10).

Greed can be categorized into these three basic types:

1. the desire for unlawful things;
2. the unlawful desire of lawful things; and
3. the hoarding of money or things

I will now cite some specific examples from Scripture to repudiate this sin of greed. Then I will use my own reasoning along with some things from other authoritative men.

First, in God's law, He expressly forbids the coveting of unlawful things. This is what the law which was delivered to Moses upon Mount Sinai says: "You must not covet the house of your neighbor. You must not want his wife, his male servant, his female servant, his bull, his donkey, or anything that belongs to your neighbor" (Exo. 20:17). That was a rule for God's people (the Jews) to follow. God confirmed this law by thunder and lightning, and other solemn deeds. He tried to impress the seriousness of this sin upon the people when they received the Ten Commandments at Mount Sinai. He wanted them to obey this law and to teach them the terrible consequences of breaking this basic, moral precept.

Centuries later, in Micah's time, the prophet complained with these words:

> "They want fields that belong to someone else;
>> so they seize them.
> They desire houses;
>> so they take them.
> They cheat a man
>> and take over his house.
> They cheat a man
>> and confiscate his property" (Micah 2:2).

The result of this theft is always misery.

In ancient times, this was also written by the prophet Habakkuk:

"How terrible it will be for those
who become filthy rich by doing wrong.
They do such things in order to live in a 'safe' place.
They think they will be immune from harm" (Hab. 2:9).

This is my point. We have many remarkable instances of this type of thing in Scripture. I will now discuss two key examples:

KING DAVID

THOUGH DAVID WAS A good man in many other respects (1 Sam. 13:14; Acts 13:22), he was tempted and he fell because he did not watch out for Satan. David was wrongly captivated by the beauty of Uriah's wife. The temptation was too great for him. He was disarmed and his spiritual guard was down. After that, nothing could dissuade David. Eventually, he ordered Joab to put in the thickest of the fighting, knowing that Uriah would not survive. This was only a ploy to make sure that David got what he wanted. It was the unlawful satisfaction of his desires. It was a way to make it look like it was not an outright murder. The plan worked. Uriah was killed in battle, and his wife Bathsheba was quickly taken in by David to be his wife. This showed David's greed. But, did it turn out well for David? No.

David's pleasure soon turned to anguish and a bitterness of spirit. His soul was overwhelmed with sorrow. The waves of guilt rushed over his head. Here is the psalm that he wrote at that time:

To the director of music. A psalm of David. It was written when the prophet Nathan came to David after David had committed adultery with Bathsheba.

"O God, be merciful to me,

because You are a loving God.
Because You are always ready to be merciful,
 wipe out all of my rebellions.
Wash me thoroughly of my guilt,
 and cleanse me from my sin.
I admit my rebellions;
  my sin is continually right there in front of me.
I have sinned against You, and You alone.
  I have done wrong in Your sight.
So, You are proved right when You sentence me.
  You are fair when You judge me.
Listen, I was brought forth into a world of wrongdoing.
  In the surroundings of sin did my mother conceive me.
Listen, You want me to be completely honest.
  So, teach me true wisdom.
Purge me with hyssop, and I will be clean.
  Wash me; then I will be whiter than snow.
Let me hear sounds of joy and gladness.
  Let the bones that You crushed be happy again.
Turn Your face away from my sins.
  Wipe out all of my guilt!
Create a pure heart for me, O God.
  And, renew a solid spirit within me.
Do not send me away from Your presence!
  Don't take Your holy spirit away from me.
Give me back the joy of Your salvation.
  Grant me a volunteering attitude to keep me going.
Then I will teach Your ways to those who rebel.
  And, sinners will turn back to You.
O God, deliver me from the guilt of murder!
  O God, You are the One who saves me.
I will sing loudly about Your righteousness.

O Lord, let me speak,
so that I may praise You.
You take no delight in sacrifices.
If You did, then I would offer them.
You do not savor a whole burnt-offering.
No, the sacrifice that God wants is a broken spirit.
O God, You will not reject
a heart that is broken and sorry for its sin.
Do for Zion whatever good You please, O God!
Build up the walls of Jerusalem.
Then You will take delight in the proper sacrifices
and whole burnt-offerings.
And, bulls will be offered on Your altar" (Psalms 51:1-19).

David was consumed with remorse. He felt that he was stuck in the miry clay:

"I am sinking deep into the mud,
and there is nothing to stand on.
I am in deep water,
and the waves are about to drown me" (Psalms 69:2).

"Pull me out of the mud.
Don't let me sink!
Deliver me from those who hate me
and from the deep waters" (Psalms 69:14).

He cried. He wept. Yes, his eyes were like Jeremiah's "fountain of tears" (Jer. 9:1).

Guilt was upon him, and his sin had to be purged! His sins were as red as crimson, and he needed to be washed as white as snow (Isa. 1:18). Finally, his repentance prevailed.

His insatiable desire for an unlawful thing (that is, the wife of another man) caused much sorrow in the life of David. Let this example from David's life be a penetrating lesson for us. Let us stay close to the cross of Christ and not stray from our watchfulness. Or else we too might be met by the enemy and be defeated.

COVETING NABOTH'S VINEYARD

MY SECOND EXAMPLE IS about Naboth and his vineyard (1 Kings 21:1-23). That field was sorely coveted by Ahab and Jezebel. Ahab wanted to annex this particular piece of property and turn it into his vegetable garden. It led this unholy alliance (Ahab and Jezebel) to such an unlawful coveting that they devised a very clever plan to accomplish it. Because Naboth would not sell his ancestral land to King Ahab, Jezebel said that Naboth had to die. She just wanted to get rid of him. In order to do this, Jezebel had some men to accuse this innocent man (Naboth) of blasphemy. She found two willing troublemakers (two sons of Belial) to give false testimony against him. Thus, in the Name of God, and pretending to give glory to God, they killed Naboth by stoning him. The news of Naboth's death came to Jezebel. Then she told Ahab, "Naboth of Jezreel is no longer alive! Get up! Take possession of Naboth's vineyard! He wouldn't sell it to you for money, but he's dead now!" (1 Kings 21:15).

But God pursued both Ahab and Jezebel with His fierce vengeance. Elijah said "This is what Yahweh says: 'Ahab, you have committed murder and stolen land! So, I tell you this: The dogs that licked up Naboth's blood will lick up *your* blood in the same vicinity!' " (1 Kings 21:19). And concerning Jezebel, Ahab's wife and co-conspirator in his greed and murder of Naboth, Elijah added: "The dogs will eat the body of Jezebel at the wall of Jezreel!" (1 Kings 21:23). Here is the infamy and punishment that comes to this kind of greed. Let this stop those who desire unlawful things, namely, the rights of others. For God is a just God. In the end, He will certainly repay such—with interest!

THE LOVE OF MONEY

THE MOST COMMON KIND of greed is the unlawful desire for lawful things, especially of riches. Money is lawful, but the love of it is the root of all evil. Even though wealth is permitted, those who pursue wealth for its own sake will fall into many temptations, snares, and lusts. Riches are very uncertain. That's why it's so dangerous. And it's very foolish to set your heart upon wealth.

Greed is hateful to God. He has pronounced great judgments upon those who are guilty of it. God once made this charge against ancient Israel as one of the main reasons for His judgments:

> "I was angry, because they were so dishonest
>   in order to make money.
> I punished them, and I turned away from them in anger.
> Nevertheless, they continued to do evil" (Isa. 57:17).

In another place in Scripture it says:

> "Everyone—from the least important to the most important—
>   is greedy for money.
> Even the so-called 'prophets' and 'priests.'
>   All of them are liars!" (Jer. 6:13)

So, this consequence would result:

> "And, their houses will be turned over to others.
> Their fields and their wives will both be given away" (Jer. 6:12).

In another place, God complained in this manner:

"But your eyes and heart only look for what you can get dishonestly!
You are willing to kill innocent people to get it.
You are making it hard for people.
You even steal things from them" (Jer. 22:17).

Through the prophet Ezekiel, God repeated His complaint against their greed:

"So, they come to you as if they were still My people! They sit in front of you. They hear your words, but they will not practice them! With their mouths they tell Me that they love Me, but their hearts only desire their selfish profits" (Ezek. 33:31).

So, in the choice of government leaders, God has made it part of their qualifications to hate greed. He could foresee the trouble that would come to society when greedy people came to power. God saw that "self" would prejudice them and that they would seek their own ends at the expense of the public's interests.

David desired that his heart would not be inclined to be greedy but that he would be inclined to the testimonies of his God (Psalms 119:36). And, in the Book of Proverbs, the wise man expressly tells us: "The one who hates dirty money will live a long time." (Prov. 28:16).

In the Gospel of Luke, Jesus accused the Pharisees of unmitigated greed: "No servant can serve two masters at the same time. The servant will like one but not like the other. Or, he will be more loyal to one and look down on the other. You cannot serve God and Money at the same time." The Pharisees were listening to all these things. They were criticizing Jesus, because they all loved money" (Luke 12:13-14). Jesus told his followers, "Be careful and guard against all kinds of greed. A person's life is not measured by the things he owns" (Luke 12:15). He went further. Christ associated greed with blasphemy, stealing, adultery, murder, and other major sins (Mark 7:21-22).

It's no wonder then that the Apostle Paul was so free in his censure of this evil. In writing to the Christians at Rome, he placed it with all kinds of wrongdoing (Rom. 1:29). To those in Ephesus he wrote something similar by adding this: "No type of impurity, sexual sin, or greed should be mentioned among you. That isn't proper for holy people" (Eph. 5:3). And, Paul urged the Colossian Christians to kill their sinful, earthly parts. He named several sins, such as sexual immorality, filthy things, and the like, but he ended with this line: "Greed is the same thing as worshiping a false god" (Col. 3:5). Or, as the King James Version puts it: "Covetous is idolatry." And we know there is no greater offence against God than idolatry. This very apostle summed it up with these poignant words: "But the people who want to be rich fall into temptation, a trap, and many foolish desires that hurt them. These things drown people in ruin and destruction. Loving money is the root of all kinds of evil. Some people want money so badly that they have wandered away from the faith. They have so painfully wounded themselves. But you, O man of God, run away from these things. Follow after faith, love, endurance, what is good, godly, and gentle" (1 Tim. 6:9-11).

The Apostle Peter believed the same thing. He called greed one of the great marks of the false prophets and teachers that would arise among Christians: He says: "Because of greed, they will use invented teachings to make money off you. Long ago condemnation was waiting for them. They will be destroyed" (2 Pet. 2:3). Jesus said in the Sermon on the Mount: "You can recognize them by what they produce" (Matt. 7:20).

To conclude, the inspired author to the Hebrews (at the end of his epistle) leaves us this key verse, along with some other things. He stated: "Don't love money." He didn't stop with this generality. He continued with these words: "Be satisfied with what you have. God has said, 'I will never leave you or abandon you.' " (Heb. 13:5 quoting Deut. 31:6).

Are we to conclude that those who are not content but who seek to be rich have forsaken God? The conclusion seems hard, but it is logical one. Some people want to be rich more than anything else. They don't want to depend on God! Paul said it best in 1 Tim. 6:17: "They shouldn't place their hope upon wealth. That is not a sure thing. Instead, they should put their hope on God who abundantly gives us everything to enjoy." And, 1 Tim. 6:6 says: "If one is godly and content, there *is* great profit!"

TEMPTATION

IT IS TRULY a reproach to a man (especially to a religious man) when he doesn't know when he has enough. God sends him one plentiful harvest of grain after another, but the man still wants more. He's so busy doing business in the world that he can't stop himself from going on and on, as if there is no tomorrow. Consider the final end of the man who wanted to build more barns (Luke 12:13-21). The more he had, the more he wanted to have. Getting more only spurred his appetite more to acquire more. In other words, he wanted to get more while the getting was good! Would he ever stop wanting more? He acted as if the creation of a surplus was the goal, not retirement. He was never content. As Christians, is that our sole duty—to make more and more money!? We ought to think deeply about the implications of this question.

It is plain that most people do not strive for a living but for wealth. Some love money so much that they spend it just as fast as they get it. Though this is sinful, it is still better than loving money for money's sake. That is one of the worst passions that can enslave the mind of man. It'll defile your soul!

This should awaken in people the serious thought of just how far this temptation of "love of money" may have already entered them! It can slip up on you. It's more dangerous than you think. How many thousands of people don't even suspect that they're already guilty of it. Those who started out poor work harder and harder to acquire thousands of dollars. Then they want to double their money and triple their money. And they spend all their time doing that (see Eccl. 2:1-11,20-23; 4:8). They do nothing else. Why? Do they just want to live comfortably, or are they doing it to be called "rich"? Look how early they rise and how late they go to bed (Psalms 127:2)? They are full of the office, the shop, the warehouse, or the business district. They are so unduly concerned about the bills, the bonds, and the taxes, etc. They run up and down as if they were trying to save the life of a condemned, innocent person. It's an insatiable lust! They are ungrateful to God who gives these riches to them to use, not to love! That is the abuse! They already have 10 times more than they began with, and much more than they are spending or what they actually need.

CORRUPTION

GREED IS ALSO AN enemy to government officials because it tends to corrupt them. Therefore, God wants government officials to be those men who are God-fearing and who hate greed.

In addition, greed harms society for older businessmen to try to keep the younger ones poor. Some people have too little, and they are forced to work like slaves to feed their families. These folks struggle just to keep their chin above the water. One reason for this is because the rich people are always holding onto what they have, and they press down harder on other people so that they can become richer. They covet more and more, and this in turn dries up the meager streams of profit for the weaker folks.

There should be a standard, both as to the value and the time of business. And then the trade of the master could be shared among his servants who deserve it. This would help the younger ones to make a decent living, and, at the same time, give the older ones time to think of retiring and leaving this world comfortably.

There is yet another problem in government. Greed causes people to

NO CROSS, NO CROWN

cheat. They hide things or falsify the goods that they deal in. Some get involved in avoiding paying their taxes, or poor quality workmanship, or even in smuggling stolen goods.

Pure greed has caused destructive feuds within families, too. Whole estates have fallen into the hands of embezzlers. Certain legal executors have kept the rightful owners from possessing what was coming to them. They won't pay them the money that they're supposed to pay. This has caused a lot of trouble for everyone and led to great oppression.

JUDAS ISCARIOT'S GREED

BUT THAT'S NOT ALL, greed will betray friendship. A well-placed bribe can undo a man. Yes, too often it kills the body and the soul. Of the soul, because it kills the life that one should have in God. Whenever money dominates the mind, it extinguishes all love for better things. Of the body, because people will do anything for money—assassinations, poisonings, telling lies, doing whatever it takes, etc.

I will end this section on greed by discussing the doom of two greedy men—Judas and Simon the sorcerer.

Judas' religion fell on thorny ground (Matt. 13:7), and the love of money choked him (Matt. 13:22). It was pride and anger among the Jews that murdered Christ, but it was greed that set that process in motion. All the Jewish leaders were at a loss to find Jesus. But they found in Judas a treasurer who loved money (John 12:6). They asked Judas some questions, and together they arrived at the price to deliver Jesus to them—30 pieces of silver, the price of a slave (Matt. 26:14-16). After the price was set, Judas betrayed his Master, his Lord, into the hands of the most cruel adversaries. But later Judas had second thoughts and he tried to return the money. But they would not accept the money. So, Judas committed suicide because he hated himself so much for the horrible deed that he had done to Jesus. Judas was his own hangman (Matt. 27:3-10).

Come on, greedy people. What do you say about brother Judas? Wasn't he a bad man? Did he not act very wickedly? Yes, yes. But would *you* have done the same thing? No, no, never! Very well, but that's what the descendants of the wicked Jews who stoned the ancient prophets said (Matt. 23:29-32), and they were the ones who ended up crucifying the beloved Son of God. He came to save them (Luke 19:10) and would have done it, if they had received him (John 1:11-12) and not rejected the day of their visitation (Luke 19:44). Rub your eyes well, because the dust has gotten into them. Carefully read your own consciences to see if *you* would have betrayed the Just One (Acts 7:52; 22:14) yourself because of your inordinate love for money. Would *you* have been in league with Judas in his sin? I speak for God against an idol (Col. 3:5). Bear with me. Haven't you resisted, yes, quenched the good Spirit (1 Thess. 5:19) of Christ in your pursuit after your beloved wealth? Examine yourself. Test yourself (Eph. 5:10; Philp. 1:10; 1 Thess. 5:21). If Christ does not dwell in your hearts, if he does not rule there, and if he isn't above everything that is dear to you, then you are "reprobates" in an undone condition! "Test yourselves to find out if you are truly in the faith. Prove it to yourselves" (2 Cor. 13:5).

SIMON THE SORCERER

THE OTHER GREEDY MAN that I want to discuss is Simon the sorcerer. He was a believer too. But his faith could not go deep enough because of his greed. See the account in Acts 8:9-24. He would have struck a bargain with Peter for so much money to get so much Holy Spirit. Then he thought he could sell the Holy Spirit again, and make a good profit from it. Had not Simon already successfully marketed himself as "the great power of God" (Acts 8:10)? He was a shaman.[1]

But what was Peter's answer and decision? Peter said to Simon, "You and your money should both be destroyed! You thought you could *buy* God's gift

1 a religious functionary who used black magic to "cure" sick people, to "divine" hidden mysteries, and to "control" events that affected the welfare of the people

with money. Change your heart! Turn away from this evil thing which you have done. Pray to the Lord God. Perhaps He will forgive you for thinking this in your heart. I can see that you are full of bitter jealousy and bound by sin" (Acts 8:20-23). What a dismal sentence! Greed tends to promote materialism, and it often rises out of it. Why? Because the more people have, the more they spend, and then they end up being poor. Self-control prevents that. They ought to know better, and there are good laws to prohibit abuses.

HOARDING

GREED LEADS TO HOARDING. A hoarder is the miser that Solomon described in Prov. 13:7. Such a man makes himself rich but possesses nothing at the end. This is a great sin in the sight of God.

But God blesses those individuals who consider the desperate situation of poor people. And then he encourages everyone to contribute freely to his brother who is in need (Deut. 15:7-8; Psalms 41:1). The Apostle Paul exhorted Timothy with the following words: "Tell the rich people ('rich' in this world) not to brag. They shouldn't place their hope upon wealth. That is not a sure thing. Instead, they should put their hope on God who abundantly gives us everything to enjoy" (1 Tim. 6:17-18).

Riches are prone to corrupt people. What makes them more generous is love. But the miser manages his wealth poorly. He "goes without" for fear of spending too much. He's so stingy. He won't spend any money because he might lose money. He is always hoping that he'll gain more money, and he's afraid that might not happen. And so he tortures himself with that recurring thought. He is very much like that man who hid his master's one gold coin in a piece of cloth (Luke 19:20).

A MISER

A MISER LOVES MONEY for money's sake. The greedy man hates all useful arts and sciences. He thinks such things are of no significance because they might cost him something to learn them. Ingenuity has no more place in his mind than in his pocket. He let his house fall apart because he doesn't want to spend the money on maintenance. And he calls himself "moderate" because of his meager diet, plain clothes, and cheap furniture. O monster of a man, you who can take up the cross for greed, but not for Christ!

He pretends to be religious too. He is always scoffing at those who spend lavishly—all the better to cover up his own avarice. If you want to bestow some perfume on a good man's head (like Jesus), then the miser will tell you of the poor (to save money and to seem righteous): "Why waste this? This perfume could have been sold for a lot of money and given to poor people!' " (Matt. 26:8-9).

But, if the poor man comes looking for a hand-out, then the miser will refuse to give him anything by making excuses about the "unworthiness" of the poor man. Or, he might blame poor people for causing their own poverty. Or, he might claim that he wants to give his money to a better, more deserving cause. He rarely opens his wallet until the day is almost over for fear that he might lose it.

The miser is actually more miserable than the poorest person. He is not able to enjoy his money because he is always afraid that he'll lose it. The miser is truly "poor" because he overvalues his wealth. He finds himself hungry in a restaurant, yet he won't spend any of his money on food! He is a wretched person indeed! He has made a god of his gold. He rationalizes that it is unnatural "to eat" what he worships.

What could be worse than somebody who actually worries himself into the grave, because all he can think about is getting more and more money. He's true to "his principles." But when that skinflint is sick, he won't spend any money to pay a doctor in order to get the help he needs to live. And so, he dies. He wanted to save money by not spending any money on medicine. He was a "martyr" for money!

THE RICH YOUNG RULER

NOW LET US SEE some other instances in the Scriptures which will warn us of sordid hoarders and those who hide their money. A handsome young man once came to Christ and asked him about the true path to eternal life. Christ told him the true way. The rich young ruler already knew the commandments of God. He replied he had kept them since he was a boy. He didn't seem like a bad person, but selfishness was definitely his problem. Here is what the text says: "However, the young man said to Jesus, 'But I have obeyed all these things! What do I still need to do?' Jesus answered him, 'If you want to be all that God wants you to be, go sell everything you have and give the money to the poor people. Then you will have a treasure in heaven. Then come, follow me!' " (Matt. 19:20-21). With that last statement, Christ hit a nerve. Jesus knew his heart, because Jesus "always knew what was in man" (John 2:24-25).

The record says that the young man was very sorrowful, and he went on his way. The reason given for this was that he was very rich. The two tides met—money and eternal life. To him, they were conflicting values. Which one would prevail? Unfortunately, his riches won out!

But what did Christ say about this? Jesus said this to his followers, "I am telling you the truth: It will be hard for a person with lots of money to enter the kingdom of heaven! I am telling you again: It will be easier for a camel to go through the eye of a needle than for a rich man to enter the kingdom of God" (Matt. 19:23-24). It was upon such rich men that Christ pronounced his woe, saying, "Nevertheless it will be horrible for you, you rich and selfish people, because you've had your comfort" (Luke 6:24).

Unless you are willing to give up all your riches and not let them be your master, you cannot enter the kingdom of God. God gives you money to help you serve others, not to let it be the master over you and control you!

ANANIAS AND SAPPHIRA

THIS NEXT EXAMPLE IS also a very dismal one. It is that of Ananias and Sapphira. At the very beginning of apostolic times it was customary for those who received the Word of life to bring whatever money they had and to donate it at the apostles' feet (Acts 4:34-35). Joses, surnamed Barnabas, was a good example of this. Among the rest, Ananias and his wife Sapphira, sold their possessions, but they selfishly reserved for themselves some of the purchase-money from the common treasury. They only brought a part for the whole, and then they laid it at the apostles' feet. But Peter, a plain and bold man, in the majesty of the Spirit, said, "Ananias, why did you let Satan fill your heart? You lied to the Holy Spirit. You misused the sale price of the land. Before you sold the field, it belonged to you. Even after you sold it, you could have used the money any way you wanted. Why did you think of doing this evil thing? You lied to God, not to men!" (Acts 5:3-4).

What followed this hidden greed and hypocrisy of Ananias? Ananias, upon hearing these words, fell down and died. The same thing happened to his wife, Sapphira. (She had been completely aware of the deceit that their greed had led them to.) Later, this was said: "The whole congregation and all of the other people who heard about these things were filled with fear" (Acts 5:11). We should learn a valuable lesson from this incident and be aware of similar evils in our own lives. What will become of those who profess to be true "Christians" but who cannot part with the least of things for the sake of Christ's cause!? Christianity is a religion that teaches people to live separately from the world and to give their all for

NO CROSS, NO CROWN

the ministry of Christ and his kingdom. Reader, you should weigh these things very carefully.

This would not have happened to Ananias and Sapphira if they had acted as if they were in God's presence. If only they had acted in love, truth, and sincerity that becomes a follower of Jesus Christ. O that people would use the light that Christ has given them to search and to see how far they are under the influence of this iniquity! If only they would guard against the love of the world and be less in bondage to the things that are seen. Concerning this, Paul wrote: "We shouldn't look at things which can be seen. Instead, we should look for things which cannot be seen. What is seen is only temporary, but what is unseen lasts forever" (2 Cor. 4:18). These things are only temporal. Then they would begin to "set their hearts on things above" (Col. 3:1-4), the things that are of an eternal nature. Their life would be hidden with Christ in God, out of the reach of all the uncertainties of time, troubles, and death.

If people would only consider how hard it is to get riches, and how uncertain they really are! Riches often results in other people being jealous of your wealth. Riches cannot make a man wise, or cure his incurable diseases, or add years to his life-span, much less give him peace in death. No, riches can hardly yield any solid benefit beyond the necessary food and clothing. The only good use for riches is to relieve others who are in distress. But we do need to be good stewards of the bountiful providences of God, and consequently accountable for our stewardship.

O that the cross of Christ, which is the Spirit and power of God in man, might have more room in the soul! That it might crucify us more and more to the world (Gal. 2:19-20), and the world to us. That like the days in Paradise, the earth might again be the footstool and the treasure of the earth, only a servant to mankind and not a god!

MATERIALISM

CHAPTER 10

"Eat, Drink, and Be Merry"

J HAVE NOW COME TO the other extreme of being a miser—materialism. It is an excessive indulgence of "self," in ease and pleasure. This is the last great moral lapse that I will attack in this discourse about the holy cross of Christ.

Materialism is a deadly, contagious disease. It creeps into all classes of people and all levels of society. Even the poorest people often exceed others in their ability to indulge in their banal appetites. And the rich people frequently wallow in those things which please "the lust of the flesh, and the lust of the eyes, and the pride of life" (1 John 2:16). Despite the strict discipline of Jesus, rich people behave as if luxury—not the cross—was the ordained way to heaven (John 14:6).

Jesus said that the following questions were the main concerns of materialistic pagans: "What will we eat?" or, "What will we drink?" or, "What will we wear?" (Matt. 6:31). He said that people without God put all these things first (Matt. 6:32). Unfortunately, these worldly worries are now the focus of fake "Christians" today. (They ought to be ashamed, and they should repent!) Those who think that Christ belongs to them ought to

NO CROSS, NO CROWN

be sure that they belong to him! They need to be like him. They ought to control themselves and live in moderation. They should realize that the Lord is near (Philp. 4:5). Fancy clothes, rich salves, bubble baths, stately furniture, expensive food, and such diversions as big masquerade balls, music concerts, theatrical plays, romance novels, etc., do not belong on the holy path that Jesus and his true followers traveled to glory. No! Paul and Barnabas said, "We must suffer many things on our way into God's kingdom" (Acts 14:22). I do earnestly urge the frivolous and materialistic ones to see how remote their current course is from true Christianity. Genuine followers ought to know how dangerous these things are to their eternal peace. May God Almighty soften their hearts to learn better. And, may He spread His tender love in their souls so that they may change their hearts and come into the love of the holy way of the cross of Jesus, the blessed Redeemer. Those who refuse to lay down their sins for the love of him cannot expect any benefit to come from Christ who laid down his life because he loved them (John 10:15-18). Neither can those people expect Christ to give them a place in heaven if they refuse to accept Christ in their hearts on earth.

GLUTTONY

NOW LET US STUDY other facets of materialism. Materialism has many aspects. The first one is gluttony. This is forbidden by Jesus: "So, don't worry, thinking to yourself, 'What will we eat?' or, 'What will we drink?' or, 'What will we wear?' People without God put all these things first. Your heavenly Father knows you need all these things" (Matt. 6:31-32). It is as if he said: "You must not live like the pagans whose concern is to please their appetites more than to seek God and his kingdom. You must not do that! But, "So, put first God's kingdom and what is right. Then all the things you need will be given to you" (Matt. 6:33).

This rebukes the materialistic eater and drinker who is obsessed with pleasing his taste buds. The glutton is often at a loss as to what to order next. He just wants more and more food and drink. He visits the kitchen often. And, his cook prepares the food in many different ways; whatever it takes to please his master. He drowns the food with various types of sauces and gravy so that it "cheats the eye" by looking new and "exotic" each time. All this is to excite the master's appetite or to impress his guests. There is great variety—and it's expensive. (The sauce might even cost more than the meat!) And, the master is so full that, even without the sauce, he can barely eat the food. This kind of eating is *not* to satisfy normal hunger. It's like force-feeding!

And, the glutton drinks the same way he eats, not to slake his thirst but for pure pleasure. All he wants to do is to please his palate. And, for that purpose, he will imbibe several kinds of spirits and liquors. He must taste them all, too. To him, variety is more delightful than anything else. The whole world is too small to fill his cellar!

If this man in his consumption had any sort of control over himself, his variety might be thought to be only a mere curiosity rather than a luxury. But what the temperate man uses as a socially-polite drink, this glutton drinks by full glasses. He becomes drunk. And he is a fit instrument for mischief. So brutal are some of these gluttons that they'll sip themselves out of consciousness. This is the lust of the flesh. It "is not of the Father, but of the world" (1 John 2:16). None of those things come from the Father; each one of them comes from the world. On top of this comes the music, the dancing, the merry-making, and the laughter.

King Solomon called it "madness":

"Concerning laughter, I thought: 'This is crazy.

Having a good time all the time is worthless!' " (Eccl. 2:2).

This is so that one pleasure may drown the iniquity of another, lest the glutton's own heart deal too plainly with him.

That's the way the materialistic ones live. They forget God. They are thankless. They abuse God's gifts and despise His counsel. They have no regard for afflicted people. They've lost all compassion and they've abandoned any sense of duty. They just go from one excess to another. Through the prophet Amos, God rebuked this very sin in the Jews:

> You blow off that bad day of punishment as if it were far off in
> the future.
> But you bring that day nearer when you hurt other people.
> How horrible it will be for you who lie on sofas decorated with
> ivory.
> You stretch out on your couches.
> You eat tender lambs and fattened, bull calves.
> You improvise songs to go with the harp.
> Like David, you invent new musical instruments for
> yourselves.
> You drink wine by the bowlful.
> You use the best perfumed lotions to anoint yourselves.
> But, you are not heartbroken over the ruin of Israel,
> Joseph's descendants" (Amos 6:3-6).

These were the vices of the wayward Jews of that day. Are they not the same vices of so-called "Christians" today? Yes, they are! Do you remember the story of the rich man and Lazarus? Jesus said, "There was a rich man who always dressed up in the finest clothes. He was so rich that he was able to feast and have a party every day.

There was also a beggar named Lazarus. His body was covered with sores. He was often put at the rich man's gate. Lazarus only wanted to eat the crumbs which fell from the rich man's table. Instead, the dogs came and licked his sores!

After a while, Lazarus died. The angels took Lazarus and placed him in the arms of Abraham. The rich man also died and was buried. He was sent to Hades and was in much pain. The rich man saw Abraham far away, with Lazarus in his arms."

The Apostle Paul pronounces heavy woes upon such people: "Their god is their stomach. Their glory is in their shame. They think only about earthly things" (Philp. 3:19).

Christ places these kinds of things in the courts of worldly kings. Such things don't belong in his kingdom (John 18:36). Such great luxuries are out-of-place among the followers of Christ. The miraculous feast that Jesus served the multitude was plain and simple. It was enough without the cook's art. It went down well because they were hungry. As Paul advised Timothy: "If one is godly and content, there *is* great profit! If we have food and clothes, we will be satisfied with these things" (1 Tim. 6:6,8).

The early Christians possessed tremendous self-control. They fasted often. And when they ate, they were thankful to partake of whatever was set before them. They learned to be content in all situations.

The disease which materialism produces and nourishes makes it an enemy to mankind. Besides the evil that it brings to the souls of people, it undermines health, and it shortens the life of a person. Through poor nourishment, the body becomes offensive and foul-smelling, lazy and unfit for exercise, much less for honest labor. The spirit being so loaded with sick flesh, the mind becomes weak. A man becomes inactive, and thus useless to society. Idleness follows materialism, as well as various diseases. Materialistic people are the burdens of the world. They are devourers of good things. As self-lovers, they forget all about God. But what is so sad (yet just), is that their end is Sheol: "Evil people will go to the grave; [1] so will all the nations who forget God" (Psalms 9:17).

HIGH FASHION

ANOTHER PART OF MATERIALISM that has a great attraction for vain men and women is fancy clothes. This is one of the most foolish, most expensive, pretentious, and unprofitable excesses that people can be guilty of.

It was shame that produced the first clothes for Adam and Eve (Gen.

---

1 Hades in the New Testament (with Luke 16:23 denoting the location where evil people end up, a place of future punishment)

3:7). Their innocence was banished, and shame became the norm . . . until people grew shameless. Today people feel as much shame to be clothed plainly as Adam felt to be unclothed!

After sin had stripped Adam and Eve of their native innocence, the main purpose for which clothes were originally designed was to cover them. Therefore, the clothes were plain and modest. The next purpose was to shut out the cold. Lastly, clothing was to distinguish genders (Deut. 22:5).

So, necessity first produced clothing. But nowadays, pride and vanity produce it. In former times there was some benefit. Today, only immodesty and pleasure reign. Clothes were supposed to be for a covering then. But today that is the least important reason to wear clothes. Greedy eyes must be provided with something to gawk at! These days it is as if clothes are made solely for decoration. It's more important to be *seen*! It's more important to see who has the prettiest dress! Today clothes come from the vain fantasies of the designers. Fashions are not designed today to keep you warm or to distinguish males from females.

The Old Testament prophets were generally poor. One was a shepherd (Deut. 34:10; Isa. 63:11); another was a herdsman (Amos 1:1), etc. They often cried out to the fully-fed, reckless Israelites to repent, to fear, and to dread the living God, to forsake the sins and vanities that they lived in. But the Jews wouldn't listen to them.

John the Baptist (the messenger of the Lord Jesus, Mal. 3:1) preached his message to the world in a coat of camel's hair. It was a rough and ugly garment (Matt. 3:4). And I don't think that Jesus Christ himself was dressed much better. In human terms, he was of poor descent. He lived a plain, ordinary life. Judging from the way Jesus looked, the townspeople didn't think that he was anything special: "Isn't it true that he is the son of Joseph, the woodworker, and that his mother's name is Mary? His brothers are: James, Joseph, Simon, and Judas." (Matt. 13:55). "He is the one who works with wood. . . . They were ashamed of Jesus" (Mark 6:3).

But it was this Jesus who told his followers something significant about

John the Baptist: "Why did you go out there? Did you go to see a man dressed in fine clothes? The people who have fine, nice clothes live in palaces" (Luke 7:25). Here Jesus was implying that his followers were not to seek after such things. His followers were to be different from the lovers of the fashions and customs of this world. He had chosen his disciples from this world and they were to be distinctive from it.

Christ wanted his followers to see how inconsistent this pompous, self-indulgent life is compared with the kingdom that he came to establish (Matt. 16:18). In Luke 16:19-31 Jesus related that remarkable story of a certain rich man. It is said there that the rich man was "always dressed up in the finest clothes." He had a banquet every day, whereas his poorer counterpart, Lazarus, was surrounded by a pack of dogs. The rich man was more concerned with his luxuries than with paying any attention to Lazarus. He had no compassion for poor Lazarus at his gate. No, his dogs were more merciful and kind than he was! But what was the end of that jolly man, that great, rich man!? It was everlasting torment (Luke 16:23-25). But Lazarus possessed eternal joy with Abraham, and Isaac, and Jacob in the kingdom of God (Matt.8:11). In short, Lazarus was a good man in Paradise, but the other man was only "important" on earth. One was poor and godly; the other one was rich and materialistic. Knowing this, people should wake up and change their attitudes!

The twelve apostles of Christ did not participate in such vain things, either. They were all poor men, too. Several of them were fishermen (Matt. 4:18-22), and one was a tent-maker (Acts 18:3). Another one was a tax collector (Matt. 9:9). So it is very unlikely that any of them were followers of the fashions of the world. Far from it. They lived poor, afflicted, self-denying lives (1 Cor. 4:9-14). They encouraged their congregations to follow their examples (Philp. 3:17; 1 Peter 2:21). Also, the holy women of those days were examples of godly self-control (1 Peter 3:3-4). They abstained from gold, silver, braided hair, and fine clothing (1 Tim. 2:9; 1 Pet. 3:3). Their adornment was "a meek and quiet spirit" and "the hidden man of the heart" which are "of great price with the Lord" (1 Pet. 3:4).

In contrast, those who live in self-indulgence are dead while they live (1 Tim. 5:6). The cares and pleasures of this life choke and destroy the seed of the kingdom (Luke 8:14), and hinder all progress in the hidden and divine life.

Therefore, we find that the holy men and women of former times were not accustomed to self-indulgence. Instead, their minds were set on things above (Col. 3:1-4). They sought another kingdom (Dan. 2:44) which consisted of righteousness, peace, and joy in the Holy Spirit (Rom. 14:17). Those who have obtained a good report (Heb. 11:2) will enter into their eternal rest (Heb. 4:9). Their works will follow them (Rev. 14:13) and praise them within the gates of heaven.

DIVERSIONS

SUCH A PREOCCUPATION WITH clothes and other types of pleasure-seeking was not only forbidden in Scripture, but it was also the background behind that lamentable message to the people of Israel by the prophet Isaiah:

Yahweh says:

> "The women of Jerusalem are so proud!
>> They walk around with their heads held high.
>> They flirt with their eyes.
> They take quick, short steps,
>> jingling with their ankle bracelets."
> So, the Lord will put sores on the heads of those women in
>> Jerusalem!
> He will make them lose all their hair!

At that time, the Lord will take away everything that makes them proud. He will take away their beautiful anklets, their headbands, and their necklaces shaped like the moon. He will take away their ear-rings, brace-lets, and veils. He will take away their scarves, ankle chains, the cloth belts worn around their waists, their bottles of perfume, and charms. He will take away their signet rings, nose-rings, their fine robes, their capes, their shawls, and their purses. And, He will take away their mirrors, their fancy, revealing linen dresses, their turbans, and their long shawls.

> "Instead of having sweet-smelling perfume,
>   they will stink!
> Instead of fine, cloth belts,
>   they will have the ropes of captives to wear!
> Instead of having their hair all fixed up
>   in various fancy ways,
>   they will be bald!
> Instead of fine clothes,
>   they will wear rough clothes.
> Instead of being beautiful,
>   they will have the brand of a captive.
> At that time, your fighting men will be killed with swords.
>   Your heroes will die in war.
> There will be crying and sadness in the meeting places
>   near the city gates.
> Jerusalem will be like a woman who has lost everything,
>   just sitting there on the ground" (Isa. 3:24-26).

O vain residents of England and Europe, your folly and your doom is upon you! Read about the prophet Ezekiel's vision concerning that by-gone, miserable city of Tyre:

> "With your great wealth and the things you sold,
>   you made the kings of the earth rich.
> But now you are broken by the sea.

You have sunk to the bottom.
The things you sell and all your crew
have gone down with you.
All those who live along the shore
are shocked by what happened to you.
Their kings are horrified.
Their faces show their fear.
The traders among the nations hiss at you.
You have come to a terrible end.
And, you are gone forever!" (Ezek. 27:33-36).

God declared His displeasure with the materialism of that reckless world then. The prophet Zephaniah continued this theme:

"On that day, Yahweh will sacrifice Judah!
I, the Always-Present One,
will punish the officers and the king's sons.
And, I will punish all those who are wearing foreign clothes"
(Zeph. 1:8).

Jesus said: "So, don't worry, thinking to yourself, 'What will we eat?' or, 'What will we drink?' or, 'What will we wear?' People without God put all these things first. Your heavenly Father knows you need all these things. So, put first God's kingdom and what is right. Then all the things you need will be given to you" (Matt. 6:31-33). Why did he say this? Because these things were opposed to the kingdom of God and His righteousness. The invisible, heavenly things are the most important matters.

Elsewhere Jesus said: "I say this to you, because you shouldn't worry about what you will eat to stay alive. You shouldn't worry about what clothes you will wear. You shouldn't worry, because life is more important than food. The body is more important than clothes. Notice the crows. They don't plant seeds or harvest them. Birds do not store their food in barns, yet God takes care of them. And, you are worth so much more than birds. None of you can grow 18 inches taller by worrying about it. If you cannot do a little thing like that, then why worry about the big things? Notice how the wild flowers grow. They don't work or make clothes for themselves. But, I tell you, even Solomon, with all his beautiful clothes, was not dressed as well as one of these flowers. Why do you have so little faith? Look at how well God clothes the grass in the fields, but the grass is here today and thrown into the oven tomorrow to be burned. Wouldn't God dress you so much better? You are much more important than the grass in the fields. Don't have so little faith! So don't be wondering or worrying about what you will eat or what you will drink. People without God put all these things first, but your heavenly Father knows you need these things. So, put His kingdom first, and all of the things you need will be given to you. Don't be afraid, little flock, your heavenly Father wants to give you the kingdom. Sell the things you have and give that money to people who need it. Money does not last, so don't trust in it. Let your riches be the treasure which is in heaven, where it will never be stolen or destroyed" (Luke 12:22-33).

What distinguishes those in the world from the true followers of Jesus? Christ's disciples are always thinking about heavenly things and God's kingdom: "God's kingdom does not consist of eating and drinking; what's important is being right with God, having peace, and being happy in the Holy Spirit" (Rom. 14:17).

Take a good look at what's here on earth. This is a fading world. You can see it written in every face. What's the point of all this buying and selling, dealing and bargaining, writing and and receiving mail, toil and labor, hustle and bustle, eating and drinking, confusion, vain clothes, ridiculous recreations, etc.? All this is at the expense of precious time! There is enough time for everybody, but time should never be squandered. We should slow down and live a plain, decent, Christian life serving God. Everything else is transitory.

Paul wrote: "In the same way, I want the women to dress modestly.

They should use good sense and be proper, avoiding fancy hairdos and gold, or pearls, or expensive clothes. Instead, use good deeds to be beautiful. Do what religious women think is right" (1 Tim. 2;9-10). And Peter added: "Your beauty must not be the outer beauty of fancy hairdos, wearing gold jewelry, or expensive clothes. Instead, it should be the hidden personality of the heart with a gentle and quiet spirit that lasts and lasts. This is very valuable before God. In the past, holy women put their hope in God. They put themselves under their own husbands' authority. This is the way they made themselves beautiful" (1 Peter 3:3-5). The Apostle Paul expressly said: "But the widow who lives for pleasure has already died (while she is still living)" (1 Tim. 5:6).

Christians should have their citizenship in heaven (Philp. 3:20), and their minds fixed on things which are above (Col. 3:1-4). "We should live properly, like people do during the daytime, not with orgies or by getting drunk, not committing sexual sin or having wild sex parties, not with fighting or jealousy" (Rom. 13:13). "No type of impurity, sexual sin, or greed should be mentioned among you. That isn't proper for holy people. You should not use obscene or foolish words. Dirty jokes are out of line. Instead, you should be thankful" (Eph. 5:3-4). "Don't let any rotten word come out of your mouth. Instead, say something good to build up what is missing. Then it will be a blessing to those who hear it" (Eph. 4:29). "Instead, put on the Lord Jesus Christ. Don't think about how to satisfy the evil desires of your human nature" (Rom. 13:14). "Don't make God's Holy Spirit sad. You were sealed with the Spirit for the Day of freedom" (Eph. 4:30). "Therefore, be very careful how you live. Don't live like foolish people; live like wise people. Take advantage of every opportunity, because these are evil times" (Eph. 5:15-16). "Try to copy God, as precious children do" (Eph. 5:1).

BE WISE!

MEASURE YOURSELVES BY THIS standard: How does your life and spirit stack up against these most holy and self-denying precepts and examples? My friends, my soul mourns for you. I have been with and among you. I notice how you live and what you do to pass the time. I feel sorry for you. I pity you. If only you would be wise! If only you would listen to the right principles! If only eternity had a little time to plead with you!

Why should your bed, your glassware, your clothes, your tables, your lovers, your theatrical plays, your parties, your treats, and your recreations possess your soul, and take up all your time, your concern, and your money? You should be admonished by one who has had his share of these things. I know that all these empty things cannot produce true and solid happiness. No, my friends, every man and woman will reap what they sow (Gal. 6:7-8). Trouble, anguish, and disappointment will be the sad harvest for you to reap for all your misspent time and money on such foolish things.

Withdraw from the world. Quench not the Holy Spirit in yourselves (1 Thess. 5:19). Redeem your precious abused time (Eph. 5:16; Col. 4:5). Stay accountable. Follow the example and teachings of Christ and obey all the precepts of his followers.

DOING GOOD

THE BEST RECREATION IS doing good. All Christian ways tend toward self-control. They are focused upon some beneficial purpose (1 Peter 1:15; 4:9-11; Philp. 2:4; 4:8). For instance, if men and women would be diligent to follow their respective callings. They would attend the assemblies of religious people often (Heb. 10:25). They would visit good neighbors who need to be edified, and they would visit the bad neighbors who need to reform. They would be careful to tutor their own children. They would be good examples to their servants. They would help needy people. They would go see the sick people. They would visit the people in jail (Matt. 25:35-40). They would try to keep peace among neighbors (Matt. 5:9). Also, they would study such commendable and profitable fields, such as navigation, mathematics, geometry, agriculture, gardening, manual skills, medicine, etc.

Women should spin thread, sew, knit, weave, garden, make preserves, and do similar, honest homemakers' chores. To leave these things undone and to do other things using the excuse of "recreation" is wrong!

WASTING TIME

SOME PEOPLE OBJECT BY saying, "We cannot always do these mundane things! Therefore, why can't we participate in harmless diversions?" But I ask, "When would you have the time for frivolous recreation?" Those who have jobs don't have enough time to do half of what has been recommended to them. And, as for those who have nothing to do, and they do nothing but sin, there is a variety of pleasant, profitable, and honorable things for them to do.

Unfortunately, with great delight, some foolish people sit for hours on end at a play, a dance, a masquerade ball, at cards, rolling dice, drinking, reveling, feasting, etc. for an entire day! Yes, they can stay up all night, reversing the very order of the creation in order to satisfy their strong desires (Amos 6:3-8). If it were not for eating and sleeping, they would undoubtedly never cease doing those vain and sinful pastimes until they die. Yet they think it is intolerable and hardly possible for anyone to sit so long at a religious gathering.

But how do these people expect to while away their vast eternity?

"A tree might fall toward the south or toward the north,

but, wherever it falls, it will lay" (Eccl. 11:3).

Let no one deceive himself or live in a dream world to think that they will be changed by a constraining and irresistible power, just when their souls depart their bodies! No, no, my friends, "Don't be fooled! You cannot mock God. A person harvests only the things which he plants" (Gal. 6:7).

But this is such a common complaint: "Why must we always dwell on these things?" Because many do not know the joy of being in the presence of God (Eph. 4:18-20). This surpasses all vain understandings (Rom. 10:2) which are darkened with the glories and pleasures of the god of this world (2 Cor. 4:4). If they were people whose hearts are set on things above (Col. 3:1-4), and whose treasure is in heaven (Matt. 6:20), then their minds would be in the right place. Those who call this a "burden" and seek to be refreshed by vain pastimes have never known God and His truth. They are declaring themselves to be most unfit for Him in another world. For, how is it possible that they can be satisfied for eternity with what is so tedious and irksome for 30 or 40 years!?

Surely those who are to be accountable for every idle word (Matt. 12:36) must not use sports to pass away that time which they are commanded to redeem. They are to make their "calling and election sure" (2 Peter 1:10).

TIME IS SHORT

THERE IS LITTLE NEED to drive away time by foolish diversions when it flies away so swiftly by itself. And, once it's gone, it can never be recalled. These unimportant things can steal your time. Who invented them? People who no longer delighted in the joys of God's holy presence. There are many excellent ways that you can spend your spare time profitably. I've already mentioned some of them.

NO CROSS, NO CROWN

LETTING SIN COME IN

IN THE NEXT PLACE, such fancy attire and wasteful pastimes show the exceeding worldliness of people's inclinations and their great ignorance of divine joys. By imitating these secular fashions and frequenting these questionable places for diversions, a certain door to mischief is opened. Precious time that was worth a world on a dying bed is lost. Money that might have been used for the general good is spent in vain. People are enjoying what they should be ashamed of. Only their lusts are gratified. Foolish are the minds of the people who are alienated from heavenly things. They are "accepted" in society by the fashion of their clothing. From this, partiality naturally arises (James 2:1-9). Denying that would be same as saying that the sun doesn't shine at noon. The acceptable, verbal pleasantries about the latest styles is detestable to God.

Also, what gaping holes these high-society practices cause in people's estates! How much are their occupations neglected? How many young women have been deceived? How many marriage beds have been invaded (Heb. 13:4)? There are so many fights, family feuds, divorces, disinheritances of children, etc. through the lack of self-control!

But of all these wretched innovations, the playhouses, like so many hellish seminaries, contribute to miserable ends. Where little besides frothy, reckless (if not directly obscene), and profane plots are portrayed, which are notoriously harmful to the minds of most, especially the young people who attend them regularly. There is scarcely a greater abomination that can be dreamed up than in those places. The more they see, the more their eyes are blinded from seeing the truth. To one who really knows God, and has a sense of His blessed presence, all such recreations are death!

TRUE FOLLOWERS OF CHRIST ARE CRUCIFIED

THE TRUE DISCIPLES OF the Christ must be crucified on this earth regarding anything that might bring them down. Their affections should be raised to a more sublime and spiritual level (Col. 3:1-4). They should behave in this world, even in its most innocent of enjoyments, as if these earthly things don't really matter (1 Cor. 7:29-31).

But if they take pleasure in anything, it should be in such good activities as mentioned before. Thus, a benefit may come back to them in some way. God is to be honored over all visible things. Each person should become an example of good, and thereby justly entitled to happiness in the present, as well as to a seat at God's right hand where there are joys and pleasures forever (Job 36:7; Psalms 5:12; Prov. 10:7,11).

CHAPTER 11

You and "The World"

MATERIALISM SHOULD NOT BE tolerated among Christians. Why? Because whatever starts it, delights in it, and pleads so strongly for it is inconsistent with the true spirit of Christianity. The very nature of the Christian religion cannot co-exist with it. Jesus enlightened us about immortal life. Why? So that we would say no to all the worldly pleasures of this mortal life. Great rewards and eternal mansions are promised by Christ (John 14:1-6). He wanted all people to forsake the vanity and fleshly satisfactions of this world. With boldness, he encouraged his followers to face the embarrassment and persecution which they were about to get from their own relatives (Matt. 10:34-37) and closest friends (1 Pet. 4:4).

If the Christian religion tolerates all that pride, vanity, and whatever might delight the senses, then why would Christians need a daily cross (Luke 9:23)!? Why deny yourself at all (Matt. 16:24)!? Why would anyone try to work out his or her salvation with fear and trembling (Philp. 2:12)!? Why seek the things that are above (Col. 3:1-4)!? Why reserve your treasure in heaven, . . . when you can have it all now!? What is the purpose of living the Christian life anyway? What does it take to receive your eternal crown? Do you think that you can live any way you please and still receive a good reward from God? No, you can't!

The Lord Jesus Christ knew about the foolish trifles, the vain pleasures, and the gross sins which so many men and women were fixated upon (John 2:24-25). He knew just how far down they had fallen (Rom. 3:23) from the heavenly principle of life into a relentless quest for the impure pleasures of this present, perishing world. He knew that people are always trying to come up with new ways of satisfying their carnal appetites (Rom. 1:30). Since Jesus saw all this, he foresaw the difficulty that everyone would have in giving up these worldly pleasures when he calls (Matt. 4:19-21; 8:19-23; 9:9; 10:38; 16:24; 19:21-22,27). He foresaw how unwilling men and women would be when they fully realized that they had to quit sinning and completely change their lives (Acts 2:36-38).

So, in order to persuade them, Jesus did not speak to them with the language of the law of Moses. He did not speak of an earthly Canaan, grand plans, having lots of children, living a long life, etc. No. Quite the contrary, Jesus spoke to them on a higher plain. He assured them of a coming kingdom and a crown that is immortal (2 Tim. 4:8). Time, pain, violence, persecution, or death, cannot separate us from God's love which is found in Christ Jesus (Rom. 8:35-39). Furthermore, he told his disciples that they would be his "friends" (John 15:13-15), his "brothers" (Rom. 8:29; Heb. 2:11), and his "co-heirs" (Rom. 8:17) in celestial happiness and glorious immortality.

Those who would not obey Moses' teachings died (Exo. 32:28; Num. 16:1-35; 21:4-6). What else could happen to those who refuse to listen to Christ (Heb. 2:1-3) and to obey the teachings of the great and eternal Rewarder of all who diligently seek and follow Him (Heb. 11:6)!?

THE ORDEAL

BY HIS OWN EXAMPLE, Jesus gave his followers a taste of what they should expect. He informed them that they would be drinking deeply of the cup of self-denial (Matt. 20:22-23). This would include cruel trials and very bitter afflictions. Jesus did not come to this earth to pave the way to eternal rest through gold and silver, ribbons, laces, patterns, perfumes, precious jewels, expensive clothes, fancy frills, exquisite dresses, masquerade parties, theatrical plays, grand ballrooms, reveling, romance novels, and other, similar distractions of the world. No! The way to that eternal rest is forsaking all those kinds of things. Yes, even some innocent pleasures. It means cheerfully undergoing the loss of everything (Philp. 3:7-8), and enduring persecution from ungodly people (Mark 10:30; 2 Tim. 3:12).

Jesus himself could have had many worldly pleasures, if such things had been appropriate for his kingdom. Satan tried to bait him with all the glories of this world (Luke 4:5), but it didn't work. Jesus set a good example for his followers to seek a better country (Heb. 11:16) and to lay up treasures in heaven (Matt. 6:20). This inheritance doesn't fade away (1 Pet. 1:4). He told them never to worry about what they should eat, drink, or put on (Matt. 6:25). "The Gentiles which know not God" (1 Thess. 4:5) are always looking for those things.

Jesus said: "I tell you, even Solomon, with all his beautiful clothes, was not dressed as well as one of these flowers. Look how well God clothes the grass in the fields! But the grass is here today and thrown into the oven tomorrow to be burned. Will not God dress you so much better? Oh, you have so little faith! So, don't worry, thinking to yourself, 'What will we eat?' or, 'What will we drink?' or, 'What will we wear?' People without God put all these things first. Your heavenly Father knows you need all these things. So, put first God's kingdom and what is right. Then all the things you need will be given to you" (Matt. 6:29-33).

The Apostle Paul wrote: "If one is godly and content, there *is* great profit! We brought nothing into the world and we can't take anything out of it. If we have food and clothes, we will be satisfied with these things. But the people who want to be rich fall into temptation, a trap, and many foolish desires that hurt them. These things drown people in ruin and destruction. Loving money is the root of all kinds of evil. Some people want money so badly that they have wandered away from the faith. They have so painfully wounded themselves. But you, O man of God, run away from these things. Follow after faith, love, endurance, what is good, godly, and gentle" (1 Tim. 6:6-11).

The Lord Jesus Christ, who taught this holy, heavenly doctrine, told each of his disciples to take up the same cross and to follow him in every aspect of their lives (Luke 14:26,27,33).

ENDURING THE ORDEAL

SO, WHO WILL FOLLOW Jesus? Who will be a true Christian? We must not think that we can steer a separate course or drink from another cup of our own choosing, different from the one that the Captain of our salvation (= Jesus Christ) has laid out for us (Heb. 2:10). No. Why? Because that was the very question that Jesus asked James and John when they were desiring to sit at his right hand and left hand in his kingdom: "You don't know what you are asking. Can you drink the cup of suffering which I am about to drink?" (Matt. 20:22).

Whoever wants to come to Christ and be a real Christian must be ready to abandon (Luke 14:26-33) every delight that would steal away the affections of their minds from the divine principle of life. They must divorce themselves from every vanity—and all is vanity (Eccl. 1:2) compared with Jesus!

PRODUCING FRUIT

A TRUE DISCIPLE OF the Lord Jesus Christ should have his or her mind so focused upon heavenly things (Col. 3:1-4) that the things of this world don't really matter (1 Cor. 7:29-31). If we have only the bare essentials

(Matt. 6:11), we should be satisfied (1 Tim. 6:8). We don't need the so-called "abundance" of this world. All we need is to have the hidden and heavenly life of Jesus. But, unless the disciple stays in Christ, it will be impossible for him or her to bring forth fruit (John 15:4,7,8). And, Jesus *does* require fruit from his followers! His Father is glorified by this fruit.

But those who live in the lusts of the world are not in Christ. They may know about Jesus, but they really don't know him. Their delight in foolishness is the very reason why they are so ignorant and insensitive to Christ. Jesus continually stands at the door of their hearts knocking (Rev. 3:20). They ought to let him in and live for him. They should know that his divine power is the cross on which every "beloved" lust and alluring vanity should be crucified (Gal. 2:19-20). If so, they might feel the heavenly life spring up in their hearts. They might come alive to seek the things that are above. Those who truly know him don't want to sin. The Apostle John said: "The person who lives in Jesus does not make a practice of sinning. Every person who continues to sin has never really understood Jesus or known him" (1 John 3:6). When Christ appears, true Christians will appear with him in glory (Col. 3:1-4). He and the Father are over everyone (Rom. 9:5). Amen.

MATERIALISTIC CUSTOMS AND FASHIONS

THE CURRENT CUSTOMS AND fashions of the world interfere with the meditations of the minds of Christian people. Worldly people are focused on this life instead of the glories of immortality. They are not revering their Creator in the days of their youth (Eccl. 12:1). They are not seeking the kingdom of God first (Matt. 6:33). They always want more than they need (Luke 12:31). As soon as they can do anything, they pursue pride, vanity, and fleshly behavior. This becomes their favorite entertainment. It gives birth eventually to wicked deeds (James 1:14-15)—lustful thoughts, obscene talk, and lewd parties. Speaking about heaven or the afterlife is tedious and offensive to such people (John 3:19-20). Asking them to reflect upon their actions and not grieve the Holy Spirit (Eph. 4:30), to consider the reality of an eternal doom (Acts 24:25), and to prepare for the final judgment of God (Acts 17:30-31) usually provokes off-color jokes (Eph. 5:4), profanity, or even physical violence.

THEIR GOAL IS TO GRATIFY THEMSELVES

THEY THINK THAT THEY don't have enough time to do all these things—bathing, powdering, primping, braiding, curling, doing anything they can to adorn themselves for flattery (Psalms 12:2). They spend all their afternoons making pointless, reciprocal visits or attending theatrical plays. They want more and more stories about romance, unrequited love, passionate lovers, disappointments, overheard mournful complaints, despair turned into joy, other surprises, speeches, secret meetings, intrigue, strange adventures in faraway places, things sent from wild deserts, daring rescues, friends and enemies and reconciliation, bloody duels, séances, etc. Things that never were, nor are, nor ever will or can be. Yet all these stories come to pass! They have everything at their disposal to dream up whatever they want. They can tell any lie—even if it is totally contrary to nature—in order to excite their minds for idle passions, to intoxicate their giddy, fictional fancies. Such things consume all their time, weaken their characters, debase their reason, and influence them to act these fantasies out in their own lives. They are trying to make each "adventure" theirs by imitation.

These seemingly innocent pastimes are actually Satan's snares to trap people. They are all contrived to have the greatest appeal to human weakness. They are very attractive to the senses. They breed vanity. Their eyes reveal their thoughts, and their looks whisper the secret inflammations of their minds which are out of control (Prov. 7:10-21). At last, this obscene acting fills their minds with lust.

Here is the ultimate purpose of the world's fashions and "recreations"—to gratify "the lust of the eye, the lust of the flesh, and the pride of life" (1 John 2:16). Clothes that were meant to cover do not cover their shame now (Gen. 3:7). They take pride and glory in what should remind people of lost innocence. Adam was wrong to seek satisfaction for himself, something other than what God had ordained for him. So it is today.

If these "pleasures" were really necessary, Adam and Eve would have been miserable in their innocence, since they did not experience any of these modern "pleasures." But they were very happy not knowing these things at all. So it is with Christ's followers who are redeemed by his eternal power and raised to the love of immortality. But men and women on this earth are still ignorant of their true rest and pleasure (Heb. 4:6). Why is there so much noise, clutter, traffic, curiosity, gadgets, pain, and so many ways to waste time and money, all to gratify poor, vain mortality!? The soul, the very image of divinity itself (Gen. 1:26), is hardly considered. Life is cheap. We're just a little flesh and bone covered with skin in a perishing world.

Those who have used their minds wrong and who are so vain in their imaginations and dark in their understandings (Rom. 1:21) not only believe they are "innocent" but they persuade themselves that they are "good Christians." And, they think rebuking them is worse than heresy! But they are strangers to the hidden life (1 Pet. 3:4). And by all these secular things they are diverted from any serious examination of themselves (1 Cor. 11:28; 2 Cor. 13:5). And, for worship, they are satisfied with a half-hour sermon, in another man's words, which has nothing to do with their true spiritual condition. Thus their hearts are captivated with this "divine" exercise, which greatly indisposes the minds and distracts the souls of people from the divine life and principles of Jesus. It's all so vain, so blind, and so very insensitive! That is not what truly makes one a disciple of Christ (Matt. 15:7-14; Rom. 13:11-12). These church-goers are totally unprepared for the coming of the Lord Jesus. They will *not* enter into his everlasting rest (Heb. 4:1).

THE CHARACTER OF THE AUTHORS

WHAT CONDEMNS THESE MANY fashions and "recreations" even more is that they are the concoctions of vain, idle, and reckless minds who gratify their own senses and incite the same wicked curiosity in others. Nothing but lust and folly are promoted by their insidious ideas. Destitute and impoverished brains use them as their means of support. They are detestable for doing this. It's a wretched way to make a living. They ought to get a real job.

It was God Himself who made warm coats from animal skins for Adam and Eve (Gen. 3:21). Were those clothes stylish? What kinds of feathers, lace-bands, ribbons, etc. did Adam and Eve wear in Paradise or outside of it? What rich embroideries or silks did Abel, Enoch, Noah, and good old Abraham wear? Did Eve, Sarah, Elizabeth, or the Virgin Mary use to curl, powder, patch, paint, wear false locks, strange colors, fancy gowns, embroidered petticoats, or did they have shoes of silk with silver laces? How many theatrical plays did Jesus Christ attend? What poets, romances, comedies, and the like did the apostles witness? No, they knew how to redeem their time (Eph. 5:16), to avoid foolish talking (Titus 3:9), vain jesting (Eph. 5:4), and profane babblings (1 Tim. 6:20), which tend toward ungodliness. Timothy was told to flee foolish and youthful lusts (2 Tim. 2:22), and to follow after righteousness, godliness, faith, love, patience, and meekness (1 Tim. 6:11).

Where do these vanities come from? From the non-Jews who didn't know God. They were the "pleasures" of such women as the infamous Clytemnestra, the painted Jezebel, the reckless Cleopatra, and the most insatiable Messalina. The memories of them all still stink! They carry with them a perpetual rot! These people were devoted to vain delights. They were not the self-denying men and women of Bible times,

The more sober of the pagan people themselves detested such foolish things and immoral behavior. Even they had principles of great virtue. None of the vanities mentioned above are to be found in Plato's works, or in the writings of Socrates, Seneca, Pythagoras, Zeno, etc. Women like Penelope, Lucretia, Cornelia, and many others could find plenty of useful things to do to keep themselves busy among their children, servants, and neighbors. Though they were nobility, they were delighted with spinning yarn, weaving, gardening, doing needlework, as well as other good tasks around their homes. They enjoyed commendable entertainment, too. Though these people are now called "heathens," they expressed much more Christianity in all their actions than do the foolish, reckless people of this time who call themselves "Christians"!

Where do you think your precious comedies come from? I will tell you. Their great-grandfather was a heathen! (And, these made-up stories were not of the best sort.) His name was Epicharmus. Though he was called a philosopher (a lover of wisdom), that was in name only. Suidas, a Greek historian, reported that Epicharmus was the first man who invented comedies. Collaborating with Phormus, Epicharmus wrote 50 fables. But do you know where he hailed from and why he wrote those 50 fables? His native city was Syracuse, which was the capital of the island of Sicily. It was famous for the infamy of many tyrants. Epicharmus' purpose was to please and gratify the lusts of some of those tyrants! Do you think that his motivation was pure? No. The origin of his tales was evil. Well, is it any less evil for someone to imitate his works, since the more sober pagans have condemned them? Isn't it abominable for so-called "Christians" to imitate Epicharmus?

The melancholy tragedies don't have any better origins than the comedies. Thespis (an Athenian poet) ascribed the roots of the custom of putting on make-up and portraying other individuals (= acting) as idolatry.

OBJECTIONS ANSWERED

BUT SOMEONE WILL SURELY say that the reason why we have theatrical plays is to censure wrong behavior, thereby teaching good lessons. And, from these we learn many worthwhile things. Now I readily admit that some of the pagans' plays helped to correct some of the common vices. That's what the philosophers intended them to accomplish. I'll mention just two examples—Euripides and Eupolis. Suidas called Euripides a learned poet who composed tragedies. And, the same historian called Eupolis a playwright of comedies. Euripides was a moral man who hated the behavior of wild women. (He had been married twice.) Eupolis was a severe critic of certain faults. The purpose of both of these writers was *not* to feed the idle, lazy fancies of people or to make money. No, the general Greek populace had become debauched, and their poetic work was to reclaim the people. The authors did so by showing that vice was ridiculous. They used their wit to speak against wickedness. But Euripides was supposed to have been torn to pieces by immoral women. Undoubtedly, it was the result of his opposition to their sin.

And, Eupolis was killed in the battle between the Athenians and Lacedæmonians. His death was so regretted by the Greeks that a special law was instituted proclaiming that never again would such poets be allowed to bear arms. Doubtless it was because, in losing him, they lost a valuable critic (a deterrent) of vice.

So, the goal of the approved playwrights of those times was to reform the people by making sin appear as abhorrent. They did this through sharp jibes and by portraying the actions of certain bad characters as shameful, ridiculous, or detestable. Why? Because, in their plays, they didn't want people to be guilty of doing the same bad things later. To me, that is a little softer than using a whip or throwing somebody into prison! Now if you will be content to be regarded as "heathen," and you would rather be jeered at than argued out of your sins, then these plays might be use-ful. But, if your lusts are strong, in no way, should you abuse the name of Jesus Christ by impudently calling yourselves "Christians"! Do you need heathens to repel evils for the love of virtue? Is this your love for Jesus and your reverence for the Scriptures intact? Do you believe that the man of God can be "perfect" (2 Tim. 3:16-17) through faith? Has all your prattle about ordinances, prayers, sacraments, etc., come to this, that you must re-sort to such pagans to be your instructors?

PAGAN OR CHRISTIAN?

MANY OF THE NOBLER pagan men and women were better taught and bet-ter disposed. They did indeed meditate upon subjects of an eternal nature. More so than the so-called "Christians" of these times! Their exemplary behavior was serious and sobering. For the public benefit the Athenian Greeks instituted the Gynæçosmi (20 men) who made it their business to observe the people's clothing and behavior. If anyone was found to be im-modest, then these men had full authority to punish that person.

But now the situation is very different: Rebuking the immodest ones is now punishable! Some people have grown so irreligious that they make fun of religious individuals. They show their contempt for all religious life by making it look ridiculous through abusive jokes on public stages. How dangerous this is!

This is the way Aristophanes treated Socrates. Socrates was once greatly respected for his virtuous life and serious teachings. But in a play, Aristophanes abused Socrates with several misrepresentations of him. This convinced the dim-witted, immoral, unstable crowd to turn against Socrates in reality. The same thing has happened to poor Quakers to-day. They have been made a laughingstock to people. Why? Because the Quakers (Friends) have severely rebuked all sin and vanity. Amid so much loose living in the world, the Quakers continue to live self-denying lives.

O blind, Pharisaical hypocrisy! Are the playwrights of today fit to be judges of religion!? They only worship the god of the pleasures of this world (2 Cor. 4:4). Their minds are so wrapped up in external enjoyments and the variety of worldly delight! You are mocking the Name of the everlasting God (Gal. 6:7)! You are deceiving your own souls (James 1:16). The wrath of Almighty God is against you all (Rom. 1:18)! God laughs you to scorn (Psa. 37:12-13); His anger is kindling (2 Chr. 13:10; 25:10,15; Psa. 78:21; Isa. 5:25; Jer. 15:14; Lam. 4:11) because of these things. You should repent (Luke 13:1-5)!

The kind of people who come up with these things and act them out are not only wicked, loose, and vain, but you are encouraging them by your patronage of their works. You could stop them from producing more plays. If the public shows that it doesn't want that kind of stuff, then they wouldn't make any more of it. These authors should be employed elsewhere in honest, useful occupations. They just want to make more and more money. And, that's how these purveyors of filth do it. If they start losing money, they invent something more titillating to make even bigger profits. They pretend that their new play is more "modern." But, in the realm of fashion, this trend-setting usually comes before the former expensive clothes are half worn. Last year's styles must either be given away or restyled into a more "up-to-date" form. O prodigal folly!

CAN GOOD ORIGINATE FROM EVIL?

BUT SOMEONE ELSE WILL raise this objection: How can those people who depend upon current fashions and "recreations" support their families? This is my answer. It's a poor argument to claim that you can do a little bit of evil yet great good will come from it. Does the end justify the means? If they have made wickedness their pleasure and their profit, then they should be content to be punished (Gal. 6:7-8). If they want to, they can learn to live without such vanities. They can find other employment, namely, honest jobs.

Just a few wealthy, powerful people create so much trouble for the rest of society. The great excess of the upper class causes the lower class to toil. If people would only learn to be content with just a few things which are necessary, then everything would be cheaper, and more people could live for less. If the landlords could curtail their expensive lifestyle, then their tenants would have less rent to pay and could prosper. Then tenants might be able to find more honest and domestic occupations for their children. The kids wouldn't feel the need to turn to a life of crime. If there were more hands making useful things, then goods would become cheaper. There is plenty of work to do in the land, whether it is in the cities or in the countryside.

If people think they'll never get rich, then they'll always have trouble in the work place. They'll never be satisfied. But those who take God's creation as their simple model can learn to be content with just a little (1 Tim. 6:8). They know that craving wealth destroys true faith. If you obtain illusive riches, they will only increase your temptations and your troubles.

DON'T BE LAZY!

THE ARGUMENT THAT THESE purveyors of excess would have no way of making a living is illogical. Should we nurse the cause instead of starving it!? No. Let those vanity vendors who've gotten rich off the people be content to retire from public life and spend their money more honestly than how they got it. Those who are really poor may be better helped by charity into better occupations. It isn't Christian to waste money on such foolish things. Public workhouses would be effective remedies to all these lazy people.

ABANDONING THIS WORLD

THEREFORE, WE SHOULD NOT measure our behavior by this world's standards. No, we testify against such extravagant vanities by our plainness and by our moderation. We choose to deny ourselves of what we otherwise could lawfully use. Overuse is common. It's abuse.

Has God given us these enjoyments on purpose to condemn us if we use them? No. What God made for man's use was good. But I have never found that living high in this world was any good at all. You must keep a constant watch on visible things so that you won't be entranced by them and lose track of heaven (Mark 13:33-37). But Christ is manifested in us, and he has given to us a taste and understanding of God. Christ can redeem our minds from the captivity of vanity. Only Jesus can entirely ransom us from the dominion of all visible objects—whatever gratifies "the lust of the eye, the lust of the flesh, and the pride of life" (1 John 2:16).

If the Devil cannot draw people directly into gross sin, then his plan is to distract the minds of men and women into innocent-looking "entertainment." His main purpose is to prevent them from doing their duty to God. He wants to take their minds off of heavenly and eternal things. Those who want to avoid these snares of Satan must think about the teachings of God's grace and His Spirit. Then they can abandon evil (Titus 2:11-15). And, by a reformed behavior, they can condemn the world of its total lack of self-control. In this way, true discipleship will be obtained. Those prodigals should remember their Father's house (Luke 15:17).

Whatever anyone thinks, the crafty Devil has never had more alluring bait than at the present time. These "entertainments" are the school and shop of Satan. He uses all of these things (fashion, sports, the theater, and other ungodly pastimes) to entice and ensnare the minds of people. He is able to totally divert the attention of people away from heavenly thoughts and divine meditations.

CHAPTER 12

Leaving "Babylon" Behind

*E*VEN THOUGH THESE VANITIES are not bad in and of themselves, yet the abuse of them is very great and widespread. They're like an infection. They ought to be rejected by everyone. Both reason and religion dictate that when anything becomes an addiction, abuse follows that. Consequently, these vanities are sinful.

Some people will ask: "Just because others abuse them, that's no argument why I shouldn't do these things." You don't want to encourage others to continue in their abuse. Give them a good example to imitate (Philp. 3:17). Telling the way is not half as effective as showing the way.

GETTING SERIOUS

EVERYONE WHO PRETENDS TO be serious ought to inspect himself. By his own example he should try to curb the lack of control in others. For example, a wise parent will take away those objects which are too strong for the weak senses of the child. Why? So that the child can be trained. The parent does this with certain things no matter how innocent the things are in themselves. Often men bend a crooked stick the opposite way in order to make it straight for later use. Similarly, those who are more serious than others should not forget what God has entrusted them with. They should exercise that same gift of God for the security of their neighbors. Cain the murderer rudely asked the Lord, "Am I my brother's protector?" (Gen. 4:9). Everybody is necessarily obliged to watch out for the best interests of his fellow man. Therefore, you should be wise enough to deny yourself the use of certain neutral enjoyments if they encourage a neighbor's folly (see Rom. 14:21).

In the Bible we find the case of the bronze serpent (2 Kings 18:3-4). God ordered that it should be smashed to pieces. Why? Because the people had become too fond of it. They were doting over it. To them it had become an idol. Yes, even the groves of trees in Canaan, however pleasant they might have been, no matter how beautiful they were to walk among, had to be cut down (Exo. 34:13; Deut. 7:5). Why? Because they had been abused for idolatrous purposes—Baalism. What is an idol but what the mind over-rates? We benefit other people when we ourselves will not use an abused liberty. People ought to give up their private satisfactions for the public good (see Rom. 14:1-23).

After reflection, no one who has any serious experience and a well-trained conscience can continue living with the same old practices of excess. What is the right thing to do? (Compare Jer. 16:5-9.) In every age, God is loudly calling out to everyone: "Come out!" To ignore this command is to fail to heed the voice of God. Come out of what? It means to abandon all the ways of Babylon—its fashions, its lifestyle, and the whole spirit of Babylon (Isa. 3:13-17; Jer. 1:8; 15:6-7; Amos 6:3-7). What is Babylon?" It is the great city of all these vain, foolish, reckless, excessive, and wicked practices.

THE WICKEDNESS OF BABYLON

THE SCRIPTURES PRONOUNCE THE most dreadful judgments upon Babylon, ascribing all the dissoluteness of men and women to the cup of wickedness that she has given them to drink. The Apostle John describes her fully in the Book of Revelation:

> "She gave herself glory and luxury.
>> Pay her back with torture and pain.
> In her heart she boasts:
> 'I am a queen sitting here.
> I am not a widow.
> I will never feel pain.'
> This is why her plagues will come on her in one day.
>> There will be death, sorrow, and no food.
>> Fire will burn her up.
>> The Lord God is strong; He judges her.

When the kings of the earth see the smoke from her burning, they will cry out loud and bawl over her. They had committed sexual sin with her and lived in luxury with her. The businessmen of the earth will cry out loud over her and feel so sad. No one will buy their goods anymore: cargoes of gold and of silver; of precious jewels and of pearls; of fine cotton, of purple dye, of silk, and of scarlet cloth; of all kinds of citron wood, of many ivory articles, and of very expensive woods; of brass, of iron, and of marble; of cinnamon, of spice, of incense, of perfume, and of precious spices; of wine and of olive oil; of fine flour and of wheat; of cattle, sheep, horses, and wagons; and of the bodies and the souls of human beings" (Rev. 18:7-9,11-13).

Behold the character of materialism and God's judgment upon it! I know that this passage contains more than its literal interpretation. It's symbolic. But one can still clearly observe the pomp, the plenty, the fullness, the idleness, the laxity, the immorality, the vanity, the lust, and the excessive materialism which reigned in Babylon. Nevertheless, on that terrible day who will go to her market-place anymore? Who will attend her plays? Who will follow her fashions then? And who will sell her delicate innovations? No one. Why? Because God has judged her. No plea will be entered to rescue her from the wrath of God, the Judge. And the Lord God who performs this is mighty (Rev. 18:8).

Since no pleas will prevent this from happening, my friends, I'll caution you (if you are repeating any part of Babylon's doom) to concentrate more on heavenly things. Hurry up and obey that righteous principle which would exercise and delight you in what is eternal. Otherwise, just like Babylon (the mother of lust and vanity), the good things that your souls yearned to own may depart from you, and you won't find them anymore (Rev. 18:14)! O ye inhabitants of the earth, lay up your treasures in heaven (Matt. 6:20) where nothing can break through to harm them (Luke 12:33-34). Heaven is where time will soon be swallowed up by eternity.

EXERCISING SELF-CONTROL

BUT MY ARGUMENTS AGAINST these things do not end here. You need to practice temperance with regard to food, and plainness in apparel, along with a meek and quiet spirit (1 Pet. 3:4) with good sense (1 Tim. 2:9) and living good, honest, godly lives among the people of the world (1 Pet. 2:12). As the Apostle Paul says: "Live wisely in front of outsiders. Take advantage of every opportunity. Your message should always be beautiful, flavored with salt. You should learn how you must answer each person" (Col. 4:5-6). "Try to live a quiet life. Mind your own business. Work with your own hands, as we told you. Then outsiders will respect the way you live. You will not be dependent on anyone" (1 Thess. 4:11-12).

And the Apostle Peter wrote: "In the same way, you wives must put yourselves under your own husbands' authority. Some of them may not obey the message, but through the good lives of you wives, these husbands will be won over without having to say a word. They will see the kind of pure life you live, which shows respect for God. Your beauty must not be the outer beauty of fancy hairdos, wearing gold jewelry, or expensive clothes. Instead, it should be the hidden personality of the heart with a gentle and quiet spirit that lasts and lasts. This is very valuable before God" (1 Pet. 3:1-4).

Paul continued with these words: "Don't let any rotten word come out of your mouth. Instead, say something good to build up what is missing. Then it will be a blessing to those who hear it" (Eph. 4:29). "No type of impurity, sexual sin, or greed should be mentioned among you. That isn't proper for holy people. You should not use obscene or foolish words. Dirty jokes are out of line. Instead, you should be thankful. You can be sure of this one thing: no sexual sinner, no immoral or greedy person (He is the same as one who worships a false god.) will have a share in the kingdom of Christ and God. Don't let anyone fool you with empty words. This is why God's punishment is coming against people who won't obey" (Eph. 5:3-6). "Don't let anyone think that just because you are young what you say is not important. Instead, be an example for believers by what you say and how you live, with love, faith, and purity" (1 Tim. 4:12). "However, we should live by the same standard we have followed until now. Brothers, be like me! We gave you a good example. Pay attention to the people who follow it. Because—as I was often telling you and I am now saying this with tears—many people are living as enemies of the cross of Christ! They will end up in hell. Their god is their stomach. Their glory is in their shame. They think only about earthly things, but we are citizens of heaven. We are expecting a Savior, the Lord Jesus Christ, to come from heaven" (Philp. 3:16-20).

NO CROSS, NO CROWN

If men and women were spiritually adorned in this way, that is, after this truly Christian manner, then impudence would soon be checked. And lust, pride, vanity, and recklessness would be rebuked (James 2:2-9; 2 Pet. 2:12). Critics would not be able to attack such widespread purity or counter such godly austerity. Virtue would be to someone's credit, and people would be ashamed of their vices. And excess would not dare show its face. There would be an end of gluttony, showy clothes, flattering titles, and a materialistic lifestyle (2 Pet. 3:11). Then innocence and simplicity would return once more (Psalms 26:6), and that harmless kind of life would be restored. People wouldn't worry so much about what they would eat, drink, or put on (Luke 12:22-31).

FOR THE GENERAL GOOD

THE SELF-CONTROL THAT I plead for is not only good for religion but politically good. It is in the interest of good government to curb and rebuke excesses. This prevents a lot of trouble. Materialism brings on weakness, laziness, poverty, and misery (Prov. 10:4; Eccl. 10:16-18). But self-control preserves the land. It keeps out foreign vanities, and it improves our own products. We don't want any indebtedness. With our proper self-control, other countries would be debtors to us. They would want to buy our goods which are manufactured here.

By this means, rich people would waste less of their wealth. And the poor would not spend so much of their hard-earned money on frivolous clothing, foolish May-games, plays, dances, shows, taverns, ale houses, and similar follies. This land is infested with such things and rendered more ridiculous than any other kingdom in the world. I don't know any other country which is so infected with cheating charlatans, multitudinous pickpockets, and professional actors (to the slight of religion), the shame of government and the great idleness, expense, and debauchery of the people. The Spirit of the Lord is grieved (Eph. 4:30), and the judgments of·

Almighty God are at the door, and the sentence is ready to be pronounced: "Let the person who does wrong continue to do wrong. Let the person with a dirty mind continue to think in a filthy way. Let the person who does right continue to do good things. Let the person who is holy continue to be holy" (Rev. 22:11). "Remember your Creator while you are young. Your old age is coming when you will have many troubles. When that time comes, you will think: 'I don't enjoy it.'" (Eccl. 12:1).

So, we cannot help but call upon everyone loudly to stand against these vanities and abuses. We testify with both our lives and our doctrine against such things. We hope that many will be weaned from their folly and choose the good old path of self-control, wisdom, seriousness, and holiness. This is the only way to inherit the blessings of peace and plenty here on earth, and eternal happiness hereafter.

OUR DUTY TO GOD COMES FIRST

LASTLY, PEOPLE MUST FIRST learn to fear, worship, and obey their Creator. They ought to pay their debts. Tenants don't need to be hassled. After the pale faces of the famished poor people are fed, and the distressed widows and helpless orphan are helped and provided for, then there will be time enough for you to plead for the harmlessness of your "pleasures." Why should the tremendous sweat and tedious labor of the farmers (who work on 95 percent of the land) be converted into the pleasure, ease, and pastimes of a small number of very wealthy men who control only 5 percent of the land? This situation is so far from the will of God, the great Governor of the world. This horrible injustice is not His doing. It's wretched and blasphemous!

On the other hand, rich people deserve no pity, no help, and no relief from God Almighty. All they do is to keep on spending and spending their money on vanity and man-made "pleasures," while the pressing necessities are ignored. This is especially true, since God has made people to be only

NO CROSS, NO CROWN

stewards of each other's needs. Everybody should help one another. See the words of Jesus in Matt. 25: "Then I will say to the people on the right side, 'You are blessed by my Father. Come, take what belongs to you—the kingdom which was prepared for you since the beginning of the world. I was hungry and you gave me something to eat. I was thirsty and you gave me something to drink. I was a stranger and you took me into your home. I had no clothes, so you gave me some clothes. I was sick and you took care of me. I was in jail and you came to visit me.' Then the good people will answer him, 'Lord, when did we see you? When did we feed you when you were hungry? When did we give you something to drink when you were thirsty? When did we see you as a stranger and take you into our homes? When did you need clothes and we gave you some clothes? When were you sick or in jail? When did we come to you?' I will answer them, 'I am telling you the truth: Since you treated some of my so-called "unimportant" brothers this way, you did it to me!' Then I will say to the people on the left side, 'Go away from me into eternal fire. You are condemned! The fire has been prepared for the Devil and his angels" (Matt. 25:34-41).

So, the powerful ones are not to prey upon the weaker ones, much less to make fun of the lives and labor of the lesser ones, in order to gratify their inordinate senses.

I therefore humbly submit this suggestion: If, in every region, all the lavish money which is being spent on such vain fashions as the wearing of lace, precious jewels, embroidery, unnecessary ribbons, costly furniture, and all that is usually consumed in taverns, at feasts, and gambling houses, etc., if all that money could be consolidated into a public fund, there might be reparations for the oppressed tenants, the workhouses for the able-bodied, and facilities for the old people and the disabled. Then we wouldn't have any more beggars in our land. The cries of the widows and the orphans would cease. And charitable relief might easily be afforded for getting poor people out of jail. Persecuted Protestants could come home from other countries. These social sacrifices would please the just and merciful God. It would be a noble example to all foreign countries and an unspeakable benefit to all British people at home.

Why should people need to be persuaded to do what would make them happy? If people today had the good sense and generosity of Cato, the Roman statesman, they would prefer to deny their carnal appetites. But it's having the heathen judge them, as well as Christian principles and examples, when they eat, drink, play, gamble, and fritter away their health, estates, and irrevocable, precious time. It condemns them!

And their final doom will prove to be astonishing, since they profess the self-denying religion of Jesus but refuse to accept his doctrine. He was humble, but they are proud. He was forgiving, but they are full of revenge. He was meek, but they are fierce. He was plain, but they are gaudy. He abstained, but they live in the lap of luxury. He was pure, but they are obscene. He was only a pilgrim on earth, but they are permanent citizens of this world. Jesus was humbly born, and brought up in obscurity. He was despised in life and hated at his death by his own people.

A FINAL EXHORTATION

O YOU PRETENDED FOLLOWERS of this crucified Jesus! Examine yourselves. Test yourselves (Eph. 5:10; Philp. 1:10; 2:22; 1 Thess. 5:21; 2 Tim. 2:15; Heb. 11:17). Don't you know yourselves? If Christ is not dwelling in you (Eph. 3:17), if he is not ruling in you (Col. 3:15-16), then you have failed the test (2 Cor. 13:5)! You are going to be rejected! Don't be deceived; God will not be mocked. Whatever you sow is what you're going to reap (Gal. 6:7-8). I am entreating you people to listen to me!

If you are enemies of the cross of Christ
—and you are so if you won't pick it up and carry it—
if you are uncircumcised in heart and ear
—and you are so, if you won't listen and open up to the
One who is knocking at the door within (Rev. 3:20)—and

if you won't resist and quench the Spirit (1 Thess. 5:19) who
  strives within you to bring you back to God (2 Cor. 5:20)
    and you are certainly doing that if you are rebellious—
then you are sowing to the flesh to fulfill its lusts, and you will
  reap the fruits of the flesh
    —corruption, woe, trouble and pain (Rom. 2:8-9) from
  God, the Judge of the living and the dead (2 Tim. 4:1) by
  Jesus Christ.

However,
if you will carry the cross of Christ daily (Luke 9:23) and
  you will sow to the Spirit (Gal. 6:8);
if you will listen to the light (John 1:9) and grace that
  comes by Jesus, the Savior, and
if you will square your thoughts, words, and deeds to be
  aligned with Christ, and
if you will deny all ungodliness and worldly desires, and
if you will live self-controlled, upright, and godly lives in
  this present evil world (Titus 2:12),
then, with confidence, you can wait for the blessed hope
  and glorious appearance of our great God and our Savior,
  Jesus Christ (Titus 2:13).

Let it be so, and escape the wrath of God which is coming (1 Thess. 1:10)! Why should you die? Let the time that has gone by be enough. "Listen! *Now* is the right time. Listen! *Now* is the day of salvation!" (2 Cor. 6:2)

Remember, you will not receive an eternal crown in heaven (2 Tim. 4:8; James 1:12; 1 Pet. 5:4; Rev. 2:10; 3:11), if you did not carry Jesus' cross on earth (Matt. 16:24; Mark 10:21)!

So, make the best use of your time, because these are desperate times (Eph. 5:16), and your remaining days might be very few in number (Psa.

90:12). So get your minds ready to think (1 Pet. 1:13), be sober (1 Thess. 5:6,8), fear God (Luke 12:5), watch (Mark 13:37), pray (1 Thess. 5:17), and endure to the end (Matt. 10:22; 24:13) "Eternal life will go to those who, by patiently doing good things, are looking for glory, honor, and life with no end" (Rom. 2:7). Then you will reap glory, honor, and eternal life in the kingdom of the heavenly Father. Amen.